THE RELIGION OF THE RUSSIAN PEOPLE

P. Pascal

THE RELIGION
OF THE
RUSSIAN PEOPLE

Translated by
ROWAN WILLIAMS

Foreword by
ALEXANDER SCHMEMANN

ST. VLADIMIR'S SEMINARY PRESS
Crestwood, New York 10707
1976

Library of Congress Cataloging in Publication Data

Pascal, Pierre, 1890—
    The religion of the Russian people.

    Translation of La religion du peuple russe, being
v. 2 of the author's Civilisation paysanne en Russie.
Includes bibliographical references.
    1. Russia — Religion.   2. Persecution — Russia.
  I. Title.
    BR932.P37213 1976   280'.0947   76-24462
    ISBN 0-913836-30-3

© A. R. Mowbray & Co. Ltd. 1976

This edition first published in the United States of America in 1976, by
St. Vladimir's Seminary Press, Crestwood, NY 10707.

ISBN 0-913836-30-3

PRINTED IN THE UNITED STATES OF AMERICA
BY
ATHENS PRINTING COMPANY

CONTENTS

FOREWORD

In the deep religious crisis of our time—a crisis which involves not only the pervasive spread of secularism but also equally pervasive and growing doubts among Christians themselves: doubts about the very essence of their faith, doubts about their vocation and role in history and society, culture and thought—the "Russian problem" has a special significance, seems to constitute a test case. The problem can be stated succinctly: How did it happen that a nation which, through the voices of its most eminent and truly "prophetic" spokesmen, laid claims to a unique religious and Christian vocation in fact became and still remains the main bearer of the most radically anti-religious and anti-Christian experiment of all times? Is this a tragical "accident for which the *real* Russia—the "holy Russia" of the great Russian prophecy—carries no responsibility, in which and by which she vicariously atones for the sins and betrayals of the "Christian world"? Or is it, on the contrary, a specifically Russian phenomenon which reveals the fallacy of the "prophecy," its wishful and pseudomessianic character? Who was right: Gogol and his Slavophile friends, Dostoyevsky of the *Pushkin Speech*, or Belinsky, who in his famous rebuttal of Gogol wrote:

> . . . you affirm that the Russian people are the most religious in the world: lie! Look more attentively and you will see that they are by nature a deeply atheistic people . . .

In other terms, is Russian Communism a Western utopia imposed on Russia, whose vocation then is spiritually to overcome it? Or is it the horrible fruit of the Russian development—or lack of development—itself?

Sixty years after the triumph in Russia of Lenin's revolution the same questions are still being debated, and, indeed, with more passion than ever before. For if the revolution seems to have triumphed on the surface of Russian life, more and more evidence is reaching us that it has failed on a deeper level. Western Christians, tortured by self-doubt and an agonizing revaluation of all their values, are forced to listen, with amazement and sometimes unbelief, to new and strange voices from Russia that bear testimony to a remarkable religious renaissance, a return to Christian faith. And again: What is the meaning of this testimony? Is it proof that, deep down in their soul, the Russian people have preserved their faith? Or it is a movement limited to a disenchanted minority within an uprooted intelligentsia?

The debate is going on, and it is in the context of this debate that Pierre Pascal's *Religion of the Russian People* must be read and heard. In it he deals precisely with the phenomenon of *popular religion* which, for more than a century, has been at the center of all controversies about Russia and its historical tragedy.

Few people are more qualified than Professor Pascal to attempt an objective clarification of the nature of Russian popular religion, an analysis of the main data and the essential facts. Born in Issoire, France, in 1890, he completed his studies before World War I and went to Russia in 1916 as a member of the French Military Russia. Intrigued and excited by the gigantic revolutionary upheaval, he remained in Russia until 1932, sharing the daily life of the Russian people, traveling, studying, immersing himself in the reality of which, upon his return to France in 1932, he became an interpreter and analyst. Fame came to him with the publication of his massive doctoral dissertation on Avvakum, the leader of the Old Believers' schism of the seventeenth century (*Avvakum et les débuts du Raskol: La crise religieuse au XVII siécle en Russie*, Paris, 1938). The book, written on the basis of hitherto unpublished and unknown sources, was universally acknowledged as opening a new era in the study of Russian religious development. Professor Pascal taught at the Ecole des Langues Orientales Vivantes, at the University of Lille, and finally at the Sorbonne. Among his abundant writings one must also mention his syn-

viii

thesis on Russian literature (*Les grands courants de la littérature russe,* Lausanne, 1971) and his short yet masterful book on Russian history (*Une histoire de la Russie,* in the prestigious collection *Que sais je*).

There is always a risk in pushing too far the distinction between "popular" and "intellectual" religion. It is for the reader to judge whether Professor Pascal's presentation of Russian popular religion has successfully faced and overcome that risk. But the richness and the importance of this confrontation to the perennial "Russian problem" and its solution is beyond doubt.

—*Alexander Schmemann*

PART I

THE RELIGION
OF THE RUSSIAN PEOPLE

THE RELIGION OF THE RUSSIAN PEOPLE[1]

To say that Russia received Christianity from Byzantium—or rather, more precisely, from the Latin Varangians, and then from Bulgaria, and only after that from Byzantium—is to say nothing as yet about the religion of the Russian *people*. For Christianity establishes itself in a different way in every nation. The sacred books are everywhere the same; but dogmas are already articulated in ways that are not completely identical, and discipline, by force of circumstance, varies still more. How then are we to think about religious feeling, influenced as it is by such a number of ethnic, geographical, economic, historical and social factors, without being bound, *a priori*, to admit that Christianity took an original and individual shape in the consciousness of the Russian people?

More to this, however: there appeared in Russia a phenomenon, which perhaps has some counterpart in Western countries, but which nowhere reached so absolute and so disastrous a degree—a separation between the élite and the people. Certainly, a rupture of this kind had taken place in France in the Renaissance era and was accentuated more and more until the Revolution. But in Russia, through the will of Peter the Great, this had been a total divorce. Peter's reform consisted in systematically creating an élite, very few in numbers, composed both of Russians and, even more of foreigners, with Western educations, who governed, commanded, and dominated in every sphere, who muzzled, and exploited for the profit of the State, the huge, amorphous, contemptible, and somewhat alarming mass of the peasant populace. This system was simply confirmed further in the course of the eighteenth century with the extension and intensification of serfdom. The result of this was a single nation with two totally different peoples, different even in language and religion.

The élite spoke French, read Montesquieu and Voltaire, saw in Orthodoxy merely a state religion with certain ritual obligations but in-

3

volving nothing in the way of belief or morality, and developed according to the fashions which came from the West, moving from Voltairean
rationalism to the sentimentalism of Rousseau, and thence rapidly to an
absorption in Freemasonry, Pietism and Martinism.

However the provincial and rural masses remained loyal to the old
customs: the true Russian language, the Orthodox faith, and often even
the 'old religion' from before the time of Nikon. They learned to read
from the Slavonic Psalter, drew their edification from the Lives of the
Saints, and listened with delight to the pious adventures of mendicant
monks, vagrants and pilgrims.

During the nineteenth century, the gulf narrowed. The élite
attempted a reconciliation with the people. A national literary language
was created, a literature inspired by the Russian people and intelligible
to them; and the people in turn received some access to Western
thought through the proliferation of schools and printed books.
Movements in the direction of a return to Christianity spread among
leaders of thought and intellectuals—the Slavophils in the middle of the
century, then Dostoyevsky and Tolstoy; and at the end of the
nineteenth and the beginning of the twentieth century, Vladimir
Soloviev and his disciples, the Idealist philosophers, the Symbolist
poets, Merezhkovsky, V. Rozanov, and the societies for the study of
'religious philosophy'. But for all this there was no relaxation in the hold
exercised by scientism and positivism over the vast majority of
educated people. And, in another way, the list we have given above itself
shows to what a limited extent this return to Christianity was a return
to Orthodoxy, how much it was mingled with elements foreign to the
national religion. Thus the gulf narrowed; but, to this day, it has never
been closed.

So we are led to conclude that there is not only a religion of the Russian people in general, but a religion of the educated or enlightened
circles in Russia, in the Western manner, and a religion of those areas in
society least affected by external influences, a religion of the people in
the strict sense of the word. The former could provide the subject for a
study on its own, in which, however, generalisations would be difficult,
dealing as it would do with groups where distinct individualities are
more sharply differentiated. The latter lends itself more readily to
description, since it deals with a mass of people, still guided by common

4

traditions and reactions. It is of this that I wish to attempt a definition.[2]

What will be the method appropriate to such a study? First, for greater safety, it will be well to circumscribe our field in time and space. My impression is that the characteristic features of the religion of the Russian people did not change much from the earliest period of which we can have any knowledge: the special property of peasant civilisation is stability. I do not believe that they differ seriously between the Ukrainians and the Great Russians. Nevertheless, I shall limit myself to Northern Russia (the most important area, both numerically and historically, and the most typical) and to the period nearest our own, that is, *in toto,* the last hundred years. I hope thus to avoid certain doubts or objections.

I should say by way of further clarification that I shall not deal with the *extent* of religious belief among the Russian people; that is a quite distinct question. I would merely wish to say that among religious people their religion exhibits this or that character.

What will be the sources of my information? Primarily, of course, a direct knowledge of the Russian people. But since no one can flatter himself that he is on terms of equal familiarity with all the people, there is no choice but to have recourse to other means.

We have those works in which the Russian people themselves have unwittingly given expression to their religious consciousness[3]—stories, proverbs, spiritual songs, apocryphal legends—and then those in which this consciousness is intentionally described. These latter are rare, and they reveal to us, for the most part, certain exceptional personalities; but equally—*mutatis mutandis*—they throw light for us upon all the others. 'The Way of a Pilgrim' belongs in this category, though it may have undergone a redaction or revision at the hands of a literate monk; and what an invaluable document it is! Its subject is a *strannik,* one of the higher manifestations of popular piety; but in his wanderings he encounters a good many perfectly ordinary personages, who are most instructive for our study.[4]

Next there are the observations on the religious life of the people made by reliable witnesses. First of all, there are purely ethnographical studies: but they concentrate more often on collecting superstitions and pagan survivals than on disclosing genuine religious feeling, and so run the risk of falsifying our perspective. More illuminating for us is the work

5

of an amateur of wide-ranging curiosity like S. Maksimov.[5] Fortunately, Russia possesses a great number of such writers, whose pride it is simply to describe the life and thought of the people. These materials must be used with caution, as they are not exempt from subjective elements; but they contain great riches; and if we find their data is generally in accord, and is also in accord with our personal experience, we have every right to make use of them. I am thinking, for instance, of the many stories of Korolenko: his interests are particularly directed towards the religious spirit of the people, showing sympathy and clear-sightedness at the same time, and he reproduces faithfully the words he has heard and the acts he has observed. Despite his talents as a writer, we may repose considerable confidence in him. Gleb Uspensky is also useful on occasion. Gorky was thoroughly familiar with the life of his people, and was by no means indifferent to their religious psychology—read his 'Childhood', or his 'Confession', or other shorter stories. However, being more of a man of letters and a politician, he requires more critical handling. One thinks immediately of Dostoyevsky; but so great is his creative power that it is impossible to consult him without some misgivings: yet that does not mean that his *Notes from the House of the Dead* is not the evocation of a living reality; nor that Maker Ivanovich in *The Adolescent* does not represent just that popular Orthodoxy we are looking for, nor that Starets Zosima in *The Brothers Karamazov* is not built up from various well-known models.

Outside the field of literature, innumerable illuminating points may be met with in histories, memoirs, travel-books, miscellaneous facts in journals, and so on. And in the memoirs of Archimandrite Spiridon, *My Missions in Siberia,*[6] we have a document of the first importance, which is at once the testimony of a man of the people to himself, and a unique collection of portraits and observations.

Finally there are the general studies which have already been made of Russian religion: but they begin from points of view different from that which I have just set out, and fail to make the necessary distinctions between official beliefs and actual religion, or between the religious attitudes of the educated classes and those of simple folk.

Notes

1. The present text is a revision of that which appeared in the *Revue de psychologie des peuples,* 2nd year, no. 2 (May, 1947) and no. 3 (July,1947), and in a German translation in *Kyrios,* 11, 1962 (Heft 2).
2. I do not want to say that there existed an absolute heterogeneity between the religious attitude of the people and that of the enlightened classes. On the contrary, we can find among the latter certain features of popular religion, but only as part of a complex totality. In order to see which features in their culture are genuinely Russian, we must begin by ascertaining which of them are genuinely popular.
3. It seems appropriate also to give some critical account of these works. Thus, the 'spiritual songs' (*dukhovnye stikhi*) are greatly influenced by literary sources (mediated through the ecclesiastical circles frequented by the mendicant pilgrims who composed them), by their verse form, and the conventions of the genre. The legends depend for their basis upon the Lives of the Saints. The apocryphal materials have their source in Greek texts. It will be necessary, therefore, to disentangle from their setting those elements which are actually of Russian popular provenance.
4. *The Way of a Pilgrim* and *The Pilgrim Continues His Way,* translated by R. M. French (in one volume, S.P.C.K., 1943, new edition, 1954; separately, S.P.C.K., 1972 and 1973). I have tried to throw some light on the origins of this work in *Dieu Vivant,* 1946, no. 6.
5. Sergei Maksimov (1831–1901), author of many works in Russian on the life of the people. The most useful for our subject are *Wandering Russia* (1877) and *Unclean Power . . . and the Power of the Cross (1903).* This latter utilises the replies to a massive investigation made by Prince Tenishev's ethnographical department.
6. *Mes missions en Sibérie,* Editions du Cerf, 1950; reprinted in 1968 (*Foi Vivante,* no. 91).

1. RELIGIOUS BELIEFS

'Double Faith' or Cosmic Christianity?

As soon as we begin to consider the religion of the people, we at once come up against a traditional and categorical assertion: this religion is a 'double faith' (in Russian, *dvoevere*),[1] a mixture of Christianity and pagan survivals.

There seem to be several which support such an opinion. There are, in past centuries, the condemnations repeatedly issued by the Church aimed at superstitions, 'vain observances', 'diabolical' festivities, and seasonal rituals: these begin, naturally, with the conversion and are codified by the Stoglav council in 1551. In the seventeenth century they are intensified around the time when efforts at reform are being made, and they have persisted, sporadically, until the present day.

These survivals are, in effect, the spring festivals, with their songs and carols in which a god of the sun, or of light, or fertility, Yarilo, seems to be invoked, and even represented; then, later, towards the end of the summer, there is the symbolic burial of this god in the form of an effigy known as Kostroma. There are traces, too, of a tree-cult. That these survivals are now attached to Easter, Petertide or Whitsun does not, it is said, alter the fact of their pagan origins. There are yet more clearly defined beliefs in evil spirits inhabiting the woods, the waters, and the house; the Rusalky are spirits of water and death; the twelve sisters called Tryasavitsy are the fevers which (as the name suggests) make men 'shudder'. The 'Unclean Power' walks everywhere, in diverse shapes, all of them terrifying. The feasts of the dead in Spring and Autumn—banquets at the tombs, to which the dead are bidden—suggest a pagan conception of survival after death.

Certain individuals, sorcerers and sorceresses, are in regular contact with these other-worldly beings: they know certain words, certain whispered charms, certain actions capable of affecting them. Their power is transmitted from father to son. But, up to a point, any man can do as much: thanks to spells and amulets, he too can summon or avert ill-fortune, can stop the flow of the blood, call down sickness on animals or humans, or drive it away. By certain procedures, or by observing this or that chance occurrence, he can predict events in which he has an interest—marriages, outbreaks of fire, deaths, the success or failure of various undertakings.

One might ask: all these practices, and a good many other analogous ones, of the sort folklorists are so fond of—do they not suggest beliefs which have nothing to do with Christianity, but which coexist with it, in the consciousness of the Russian peasant, and adulterate it? Are they not as typical instances of *dvoevere* as the magical recitations disguised as exorcisms which we find, for example in the story of St Tryphon?

We may note, to begin with, that Tryphon's exorcism has a Greek, not a Russian, source,[2] though the source is hardly important. What must be determined is the place occupied by these superstitions in the life of the Russian people, not five hundred years ago but today, and, further, the kind and the degree of belief accorded them. It is certainly noteworthy that, even in the seventeenth century, a man like Archpriest Avvakum, coming from a township (now vanished) in the Nizhni-Novgorod district, an area then only recently colonised, presents to us in his writings, his life, letters, and sermons, an absolutely pure form of Christianity, without the least trace of 'vain observance' or the faintest reflection of paganism. It is true that he was an extraordinary man: but his education and his life had been entirely among the people. Would he not have preserved some shadow of 'double faith' if it had really existed? The abuses which he fought among his parishioners were failures in devotion or morality—the obscene performances of the bear-wards, or the masquerades of Carnival time: they are characterised as devilish and pagan, but the good folk who enjoyed them did not see their faith as being in any way involved.

Similarly, in all the scenes which Melnikov-Pechersky[3] relates with such delight, scenes of divination, garlands hung in the trees, effigies drowned to the accompaniment of carols and songs, the part played by pagan belief seems to be completely submerged in the dominant feeling of sport, play. After all, do the young peasant girls—not to mention the young ladies of the towns as well who, on the night of 31 December, read their fortune for the coming year in the grotesque patterns made by wax in contact with boiling water—do these show any more 'double faith' than the Frenchwoman who goes to have her fortune read in the cards or is afraid of seeing three lamps burning together.[4]

The only pre-Christian element which long remained alive in the faith of the Russians (and still remains so, at an implicit level) was the belief in the power and sanctity of the Earth. And this, properly speaking, is a feeling which is 'natural' rather than strictly pagan: the earth which nourishes, the earth, whose inexhaustible energy spends itself and is mysteriously renewed year by year, the earth which sustains man, and in which at the end he comes to rest—how could this not be, for an agrarian folk, 'the moist Earth our mother'? It is not personified nor divinised, neither surrounded with legends nor honoured with worship: that would truly be paganism. But it is felt that it is pure and that nothing unclean should tarnish it. This is why the boyarina Morozova, an educated Christian lady and a rigorously observant spiritual daughter of Archpriest Avvakum, when she thought that she was going to die in prison, requested a soldier to wash the one shift she possessed, because 'it would be unfitting for this body to go down in an unclean garment into the bosom of its mother the earth'. Out of respect for the earth, every peasant keeps throughout his life a costume for death: a white shift and slippers of bast. Even working on the land should only be done in a state of physical and moral purity. The earth is taken as witness to an oath. Even more strikingly, before confessing his sins to the priest, the peasant asks pardon from his neighbours and from the earth as well.

When there is no priest available—as often happens in the North or in Siberia—the Orthodox believer makes his confession directly to the earth; as does, with much stronger cause, the 'priestless' Old Believer for whom the grace of the priesthood has been withdrawn from the world science Nikon's time.

It is by no means easy to say to what extent this belief in the sanctity of the earth is present in the consciousness of the Russian people today. But some evidence on various related points has been collected since the beginning of the century. Have we here a case of paganism and 'double faith'? I believe rather that what we are dealing with here are certain authentically Christian features of popular religion. The peasant, together with Genesis and St Paul, believes that the whole creation, which the Earth represents, is affected by man's sin and called to renewal with him. His religion has hardly any conception of individual fall and individual salvation: it is more collective, cosmic, never forgetful—as the West has tended to be—of the great visions of the Apocalypse. It is on that level that it exists. It is powerfully aware of a mystical communion between man and nature, both alike works of a good God. Nature is always pure. Man, when he sins, separates himself from it and sees no more than what can be seen from the outside. But the pure man perceives its beauty, its oneness with God and his own oneness with it. The Pilgrim, once he has entered the state of perpetual prayer, sees everything around him in a fresh and wonderful light—trees, plants, birds, earth, air, sunlight, everything proclaim's God's love for man, everything prays and sings of the glory of God. The Missionary too, in his childlike purity, receives his earliest call to prayer from nature. Makar Ivanovich who, in *The Adolescent*, stands for popular religion at its higher levels, sees the mystery of God in all its fullness, an indescribable beauty, shining in every blade of grass, in the singing of the birds and in the stars. After the accusation of paganism should we now press the charge of pantheism? The Russian believer would be surprised if we did; for, if nature puts him in contact with God, it is not through any confusion with God, but because nature is his creation.

The Christian value of such popular intuition has been so fully acknowledged by various thinkers that writers and theologians have tended to exploit it, to draw it out and examine it in depth, to what is perhaps a rather excessive degree. Raskolnikov in *Crime and Punishment* and Alyosha in *The Brothers Karamazov* kiss the earth which they have polluted and afterwards experience the sensation of having been absolved and reconciled with God. Starting from various hints to be found in the spiritual songs (which are only partially an expression of popular belief), Dostoyevsky, with the help of the character of the crippled girl in *The Possessed*, builds up an analogy between Mother-Earth and the Mother of God. Later on, Fr Sergei Bulgakov expands this still further, and adds his 'sophianic' conceptions to this complex of ideas. But the pure and straightforward cosmic sense of the peasant is more sober and less easy to discuss; never does it contradict the

11

Orthodox faith.

Before she goes to the church to make her confession, a peasant woman of whom S. Smirnov tells us discharges herself of a number of preparatory actions. She makes her peace first with her family, and then addresses the whole of nature: the fair sun, the clear moon, the numberless stars, the dark nights, the soft showers, the raging wind, and then, at greater length, the earth. She recites these lines:

> Moist mother earth, I shed my tears upon you,
> Moist earth that nourishes me and gives me drink,
> I am a worthless foolish sinner,
> For my legs as they walk trample you down,
> And I have spat out sunflower seeds upon you . . .
> My arms in their vigour have tossed you away,
> My eyes have rested their gaze on you.

She stops to purify her hands by rubbing them with earth—or, in winter, snow, but a handful taken from deep down—and resumes her recitation with a deep bow:

> One further blow, my foster-mother,
> I wish to touch you with my head,
> To beg your blessing,
> Your blessing and your pardon.
> I have torn up your breast
> Cutting with the iron ploughshare.
> Never have I smoothed your surface with a roller,
> Never combed your locks with a comb:
> I have bruised you under the harrow
> With its teeth of rusty iron.
> Foster-mother, pardon me,
> In the name of Christ our Saviour,
> Of the Holy Mother of God,
> Of Blaise our intercessor,
> Elias the wise, the prophet,
> And the knightly George.[4]

When we have come to this point, it is surely legitimate for us to interpret those seasonal rituals which have caused us some uneasiness, as being, from a very long time back, no more than an expression of this same communion which the country people felt to exist between themselves and that 'nature' which the good God had made. Among Melnikov—Pechersky's Old Believers, it is quite clear that it could be nothing else.

In spite of everything, the cult of the Earth and the seasonal festivals are no more than survivals. Aprt from this, in general terms and in daily life, did the Russian people have a theology of their own? As regards the Trinity—did they admit side by side with some unknown divine essence, something like two principles, male and female, Christ and the Mother of God? Did they submerge Christ the Saviour in Christ the King and Judge? These again are features which we notice in the spiritual songs, but which are elsewhere contradicted. Very often Russia has simply been ignorant about dogma: a pessimistic priest in 1857 tells us that 'two-thirds (of the peasants) have not the least idea of the faith' and hardly ten per cent can recite the Creed. Whence, then, does their religious belief derive? In a limited degree, from instruction at school; but far more so, from the tradition handed on in the family, and from various books, read singly or together (the maxims contained in the old primers, the Bible, especially the Psalter and the Gospel, the Lives of the Desert Fathers and the Saints, and contemporary tracts), from the Liturgy, with its prayers, scriptural readings and hymns, from preaching, pilgrims' stories, religious paintings, and the 'apocryphal' narratives on the borders of the Old and New Testaments.

Such diverse and random sources cannot provide an explicit and confident acquaintance with the truths of Christianity; but they are enough to give some satisfaction to the enormous intellectual curiosity of this nation. If the Russians generally, are content—like the great mass of the faithful in every land—with an implicit and comprehensive faith, may there not be certain mysteries which attract their deeper interest?

Among such matters, it seems to me, are the Last Things. It is well known how readily the Russians have believed in the imminent end of the world during every period of disturbance in their history: at the time of the great schism of 1666, during Peter the Great's reforms, and in our own day. The relevant texts are ever present in their memory, they recognise the signs, the marks of Antichrist. Whole parishes have been known to take to flight, abandoning everything, either letting themselves die or preparing themselves to appear, trembling but pure, before their Judge. Scenes of the Last Judgement and scenes from the Apocalypse are depicted over the doors of churches and monasteries, and crowds gather in front of them before and after services. The Pilgrim tells us of a foul-mouthed, drunken labourer who was converted by listening to a discourse of the Last Judgement. Also, the Russian finds in this dogma of final retribution a solution to the problem which torments him, the problem of evil and suffering; in the Resurrection he sees the conquest of death, and both death and resurrection are understood in a universal sense: the animals too have a sort of unbaptised soul which will appear in the other world. However, in this self same dogma, popular thinking encounters its great scandal, the eternity of the pains of Hell—evil and suffering yet again, and this time infinitely prolonged. And so, with relief, it seizes on all the available compromises: the holy Virgin, by the power of her intercessions, has secured for the damned a remission of their pains every year from Maundy Thursday to Pentecost;[6] so great a feast is the Annunciation that the inhabitants of Hell are not tortured on that day; the bell rung for the soul of a suicide calls him out of Hell for as long as it is ringing . . . These very widespread beliefs so clearly satisfy a need in the Russian soul that even some theologians willingly revert, on this question, to the merciful opinions of Origen and Gregory of Nyssa.

Another point on which the Russians have reflected is the universal presence of God and his Providence. In all the events of life, they discern the workings of this Providence. There is not fatalism in this, as is sometimes alleged, for the Russian peasant has his equivalent of the proverb, 'Heaven helps those who help themselves', and is no less courageous in his efforts than any other peasant in the world. He is aware of his freedom. Nevertheless, he lives also on a higher plane in a higher atmosphere, where the Devil lies in wait for him, but where God too watches over him. Other proverbs bear this out: 'Who shall help us, if not God?', 'Hope in God, and do not accuse others!', 'No cudgels against God', 'Our will is nothing without the will of God', 'Without God, how can you so much as cross your own threshold?' In the autobiography of Avvakum, in the Pilgrim and the Missionary, this providential at-

14

mosphere is most pronounced: but in some degree the humblest *muzhik* always feels himself enfolded in it.

Concern with Heaven, Hell, and the world to come, and a direct sense of the divine ordering of things are, once again, characteristics of a religion which encompasses all the dimensions of the universe. But could it be said that, in its worship, it restricts itself to empty ritualism?

Notes

1. We shall not use the word 'dualism', to avoid confusion with Manichaean dualism (of which also some have claimed to find traces in the religion of the Russian people).
2. I have found Tryphon's exorcism in a recent *Lesser Euchologion* published in Athens. The humble Tryphon adjures the earthworms, cockchafers, grasshoppers, lice, fleas and slugs to leave the fields, gardens, fruit-trees and vines and go back to the wild mountains, and the dry and barren places, if they do not want him to call up against them the angel of the Lord to kill them or the sparrows to eat them up.
3. In the novel *In the Forests (Dans les Forêts),* superbly translated by Sylvie Luneau, Paris, 1957. It deals with the Old Believers of the Trans-Volga region, to the north of Nizhni-Novgorod.
4. The study of superstitious practices has advanced quite a long way in Russia since the last century. S. Tokarev, *Religious Beliefs of the Eastern Slavonic Peoples in the Nineteenth and Twentieth Centuries,* Moscow, 1957 (Academy of Sciences) has provided an exhaustive account, with an attempt at classification. He defines religious beliefs by their acceptance of a 'supernatural', but, in fact, does not discuss religion properly so called at all.
5. Prof. S. Smirnov, in *The Confessor in Old Russia,* Moscow, 1914, pp. 255–283, devots his *Appendix II* to 'Confession to the Earth'. In French some reflections of the cosmic aspect of Russian religion may be found in L. A. Zander's little book, *Dostoïevski: le problème du bien,* Paris, 1946.
6. This is the subject of the apocryphon, *The Pilgrimage of the Mother of God Among the Torments of Hell,* the text of which may be read later in this book.

2. WORSHIP

Idolatry or Symbolism?

Foreign travellers over the centuries, Russian intellectuals, and, at the present time, the official propagandists of atheism, unite in condemning popular religion as mere formalism, devoid of genuine piety, a kind of idolatry.

They turn their attention first to the worship of images. The icon has an immense rôle to play: it is to be found in multiplicity in the church—on the iconostasis, displayed in three tiers or more, on walls, pillars, and desks. It is to be found by the roadside and at crossroads, and at the entry to villages, over doors, inside houses, in every room, in the place of honour facing the door, so that anyone coming in greets it at once.
facing the door, so that anyone coming in greets it at once.

This corner with the icons—sometimes ten or twenty of them on shelves—is almost a little household chapel: you also put there the things you are most fond of; a lamp burns there, at least on feast-days; and you pray in front of it. The icon goes with a man for the whole of his life: he receives it at baptism, it is carried at the head of his wedding procession, and it goes before him at his burial. Parents use it in giving their blessing to those going on journeys, or to newly-wed couples, and at the moment of departure from this life, to all those standing by.

A whole pattern of worship is organised around the icon. It is kissed devoutly: an old woman in Moscow, at the end of every service, used in this way to kiss all the images she could reach, and then, from the middle of the church, would blow kisses with her hand to the others.[1] She was in that respect a woman of the people, though to a rather exaggerated degree.

Some icons have a history or a legend, and receive public homage: they are carried in procession, or—still in procession—parishes come out to venerate them, with their banners (which are also themselves icons)

16

borne before them. These processions are major manifestations of popular religion: the progress of the icon may last for several days, even whole weeks; the bearers of the icon and the accompanying pilgrims are organised in relays from one village to the next; songs are raised, ecstatic worshippers prostrate themselves, kiss the earth and beg as a favour that the icon should pass over their bodies. Demoniacs rave, women show signs of hysteria. Korolenko has described some of these scenes.[2] Such mass demonstrations are easily turned to political ends: sometimes they precede pogroms; in the last days of the Empire, they served the mysterious purposes of an unbalanced monk named Iliodor. But these happenings were abuses and exploitations of a perfectly genuine popular feeling.

When the workers of S. Petersburg—tens of thousands of them, with their wives and children—resolved, on the 9th (N.S. 22nd) of January, 1905, to take their grievances to the Tsar, the holy images went before them, to stress the serious and near-religious character of their procession; for the icon presides over political as well as domestic life. They were met with rounds of gunfire. The Tsar had not understood, and this was, for them, the revelation of a bottomless pit: what was this authority which has no respect for the icons?[3]

The icon is highly potent. To protect your *izba* when the village is on fire, you walk around it with the icon of Our Lady in the Burning Bush: you most hold it in your hand while you look at the fire. A group of workers dissatisfied with their employer, having exhausted all earthly means of appeal against him, drew up a fresh complaint and deposited it before a much revered icon of the Virgin.[4] The icon is holy. It is not to be moved unnecessarily or disrespectfully; you should not put your feet up in its presence; if it becomes unusable, all you can do is to leave it to the elements—put it in the earth, or in running water, or consign it to the fire. In the sight of the icon, nothing impure should be done: it must at least be veiled (hence the expression: 'Time for the icons to go out!').

Do we not have here all the elements of idolatry? Superficial observers may have been mistaken about this; but it must be acknowledged that the danger of formalism is not absent. In early Byzantium (whence the cult of images derives), several holy persons testify to this: thus the Iconoclast movement arose. But man is not pure spirit; he needs tangible representations which evoke for him realities

17

inaccessible to his senses. Thus the Greek Church allows images, while stating very precisely their value as symbols. The Russian peasant is no theologian, who can distinguish the different kinds of worship, *latria, hyperdoulia,* and *doulia*; but for his own part, when he speaks of the 'gods' of his domestic chapel, his use of the word is not innocent of irony. He knows quite well who it is who is present behind this bit of painted wood. The painting is, indeed, done in such a way as to suggest an ideal being, removed from everyday, fleshy life: an icon is quite the opposite of a portrait. What the believer sees through it, what he kisses, petitions or thanks, is the person of the Saviour, the Virigin, or the Saint. He does not say: 'The image of the Virigin is going forward on its litter', but 'The Most Holy One goes forward!' If a miracle is worked by an icon, a healing of soul or body, a material favour, he does not imagine that this icon itself is responsible: it is purely the occasion or the channel for it; the grace of God works through it. This is the doctrine, and this is the conviction even of the simplest folk, when they reflect on it; it is this which Seraphim of Sarov, who was so close to the people, expresses.[5] They are not divinising material things, but they need them in order to come into contact with the immaterial world. In the same way, philosophy requires human concepts if it is to think analogically about divinity.[6] If particular abuses can be introduced into the cult, that is only natural; but it should not be allowed to tarnish in our eyes the authenticity of popular intuition. Anyone who, in Kiev or elsewhere, has seen pilgrims praying before the icons for long periods, as if in ecstasy, will make no mistake about this. And, on the other hand, when the Soviet authorities compelled the peasants to bring their icons to be burned on huge bonfires, not one of them failed to understand, in spite of their bitter sorrow, that this was not something affecting the heart of their faith.

The icon is, then, in Catholic terminology, a sacramental. We must recognise that Russian piety makes extensive use of sacramentals, revering and, according to custom, kissing the relics of the saints, certain of which are specially honoured and are consequently objects of pilgrimage. One thinks immediately of the many bodies of hermits preserved in the subterranean galleries, 'Inner' and 'Outer', of the Lavra at Kiev. Other objects too serve as vehicles of grace: the oil in the lamps which burn in front of certain icons or relics, water from the wells of cer-

18

tain monasteries, the baptismal cross which every Russian must wear at his breast—more than a symbol, it is the very mark of his Christianity. And the sign of the cross is a powerful thing. So too is the blessing of father or mother; and it is indispensable in serious circumstances. It is the viaticum which parents leave to their children on their deathbeds. A young orphan girl, engaged to be married, will go to her parents' tomb on the eve of her wedding to ask their blessing.[7] A parental letter to a soldier serving in Finland during the last war ended with these solemn words: 'Dear son Grigori Leonovich, we send you a father's and a mother's blessing, to abide with you there inviolably for ever'.[8] Refusing a blessing is a burden for the conscience; cursing is almost a token of damnation.[9]

Modern man in the West has reduced the outward signs of religion to a minimum in his daily life. The Russian peasant greets the icons on rising. When he leaves his house in the morning he signs himself three times, looking first towards the church or chapel, then towards the East, then the four points of the compass, to give thanks to the Creator. He takes no food without making the sign of the cross. From time to time he will murmur the ejaculatory prayer, 'Lord Jesus Christ, Son of God, have mercy on us', or simply, 'Lord Jesus Christ'.

He multiplies his signs of the cross, genuflections, invocations, and all such exterior manifestations, untroubled by the least consideration of human respect, to the point of giving the impression that these are mechanical exercises without interior reality. However, it would be a mistake to think this: while they may not necessarily express authentic devotion, they do correspond to an habitual disposition.

There is a kind of 'ritual of labour', in which the saints play a considerable role: Boris and Gleb must be invoked before the autumn sowing, which must be completed for their feast-day. The Russian people, like others, allow special functions and concerns to the saints: Basil is the protector of pigs, Cosmas and Damian cure the ailments of poultry, Zosimus is associated with bees, Jeremiah looks after tools, Florus and Laurus are guardians of horses, Anastasius keeps a favourable eye on sheep; and there are many more such. At the root of these peculiarities lies sometimes an adaptation of the functions of pagan deities, sometimes a joke based on a pun or a popular etymology, or, most often, the memory of some episode in the life of the saint in

19

question. If there is superstition here, it is no more marked than the sort we meet in other lands. But is this not rather an embellishment of the patterns of life—every action tied to some ceremony, so many days lifted out of the general monotony, every job devoutly allocated its patron saint and so enriched with significance? However, could it not be said that the saints come to eclipse their Lord? Not at all: the peasant does not forget that there is a master above the servants. The fisherman of Baikal or Obi do not leave the shore before the *bashlyk* or head of the *artel* has said, 'Lord, bless us!' Before fixing the net in place, the *bashlyk* says 'Hear our prayer!' All stand, take off their caps and reply, 'Say the prayer!' The *bashlyk* repeats the prayer of Jesus and all reply 'Amen'. The *bashlyk* says 'Have mercy!' then all say at once, 'God be our helper!' Only then do they set sail. 'God help you!' is the greeting given by the passer-by when he sees someone working. The first fruits of the herd, of the soil or the trees are dedicated to the Creator: you do not eat honey before the 'first day of the Saviour' (1 August), nor do you eat apples or green peas before they are offered at the altar on the 'second day of the Saviour' (the feast of the Transfiguration). This is nothing to do with the saints: God himself is the master of the seasons and the crops: 'If God does not so will, the earth itself will not bring forth. God gives the rain and gives the grain as well.'

These are peripheral observances. What of the main cult, with its special ministers and special setting, the clergy and the churches? It should be said at the outset that the Russian people have not established the distinction between the church and other, secular places that we are accustomed to in modern times. The *izba* has its corner with icons, an honoured place which is almost sacred; and the church has only one absolutely sacred spot, the Holy of Holies, the altar draped in the *antimins*. Similarly, there is no gulf of celibacy between priest and layman; the deacon is nearer still to the peasant; though, on the other hand, even the sacristan is already a cleric of sorts.

The clergy are very far from playing as essential a part here as they do in Western religion. There is an important geographical reason for this: the country parishes are very few in number, and it is by no means unusual for one to serve twenty or thirty hamlets within a radius of forty or fifty versts. So it is very often necessary to do without the priest. In the district of the Olonets, burials are carried out without him, and the funeral pall is later taken to him, when opportunity arises, for his blessing. The Liturgy, the Mass, then comes to be replaced by domestic ceremonies: the head of each family reads prayers and psalms and censes the icons. And so, by force of circumstances, the Orthodox are not much different from the priestless Old Believers.

A further reason for the fact that pastors are so very close to their flocks is that the 'distance' necessary for respect is lacking, as also is any superiority of an intellectual or moral sort. This is the place to mention the allegations of drunkenness and using the sacraments for financial profit. Hence those proberbs, anecdotes and insulting expressions which plausibly suggest a deep-rooted anticlericalism: it is a bad omen to meet a priest when coming out of the house—cross your fingers, avert your eyes, there's the parson. You must try and live well here on earth so as not to end up side by side with the parsons in Hell. St Peter's Lent was invented by parsons and women (for the latter to hoard their butter and the former to keep up the collections in church). We should not give these remarks and caustic aphorisms any more importance than does the peasant himself. He is fond of a joke; and all peoples are—quite reasonably—very demanding towards those whom they expect to set them a good example.

We can only conclude that Russian popular religion is about as unclericalist as it could be, not in any way tied to the clergy. It would not cross the peasant's mind to abandon the church and the sacraments because he thought his priest unworthy. The inadequacy of the clergy will never put his faith at risk. Similarly, this religion is as little as possible tied to the church. It can be practised, if circumstances so dictate, in the humblest oratory or simply at home. It is to the house that the priest comes to give a blessing, to baptise, or to conduct one of those private services known as *moleben*—whether as a thanksgiving, or a supplication, or out of a simple devotion. When there is neither church nor priest, the head of the family can conduct a simplified form of worship at home. The explanation of this feature of popular religion is the general disdain in Russia for absolute division, prohibitions and precepts: why have watertight partitions between divine and profane? And, in practice, this has had some very important results: because neither church nor clergy were felt to be indispensable, then, when priests were deported and churches demolished or converted into shops or cinemas, it was enough to keep alive the link with the Church that a priest in disguise should pass through at long intervals, baptising the children of the district, and blessing wedding-rings or burial-grounds.

This does not mean at all that the Russian peasant comes anywhere near rejecting public worship and priesthood. Quite the contrary; he loves 'the good Lord's churches', where everything delights his soul and his senses—the bells with their sound 'like summer fruit',[10] the bright colours of the murals and the harmonious lines of the exterior, the huge icons of the Saviour and the aspostles painted under the domes, the stories from Old and New Testaments depicted on the pillars and the iconostasis, the warmth of the candles, the heady fumes of incense, the embroidered decorations—in short, all the splendours of the Liturgy. All this he loves; and even more he loves the chant, in which the various tones of the human voice—unaccompanied by any instrument—ring out with the most exalted meditations and the most poignant sentiments. There must be a deacon with a deep bass voice to give out the acclamations, while the priest must have a soft and moving voice for the words of mystery. There must be a well-provided choir, well-conducted and well-rehearsed. The Russian people are too sensitive to beauty not to appreciate the Liturgy, the only perfect beauty on earth. Reading the life of this or that holy person, you notice the part played in his devotion or his conversion by the Liturgy: there is no need to go all the way back to Vladimir's ambassadors, so enthralled by the ceremonies at Hagia Sophia that they wondered whether they were still on earth.

And furthermore, the Russian people multiply occasions for enjoying this beauty: they have never invented the Low Mass, and every Eucharist is sung. They have preserved the celebration of the evening office on the eve of Sundays and feast days; and there are many feasts, of the Saviour, the Virgin, the apostles, the patron saint, solemnly kept in the church as in the whole community. A new feast is created in a parish to commemorate a miracle which has been granted, with office, procession, and general celebration . . .

In the Slavonic Liturgy, not everything is intelligible to the simple folk, and there are no books to translate it for them. But the Slavonic is closely related to Russian, and as a result of this the essential parts of the offices are understood. Thus, the Liturgy in itself is one of the most efficacious sources of belief (the Creed), of piety (the Lord's Prayer) and of ethics (the Beatitudes sung during the Mass). And there are the readings from the Gospel, the hymns, and the special ceremonies of Holy Week and Easter. Here again, then, it would be wrong to speak of exterior observances, empty and purely aesthetic—another reproach often formulated by superficial observers.

The Russian people know that there is meaning and substance beneath the forms of ritual and chant. How else could we explain the respect and gravity surrounding the sacraments? When a sick man has received extreme unction, he must, if he recovers, consider himself to be no longer of this world, and to to live as a monk or recluse.[11] Although confession is often simplified excessively, despite the prescriptions of the Ritual (doubtless because of the negligence of the clergy) is still obligatory before communion. Further preparation for communion takes the form of a sort of retreat, a *govenie*, involving a week's attendance at the offices, fasting and spiritual reading—in short, an attempt at perfection. In these conditions, it occurs only rarely, during one of the Lents, principally in the Great Lent. This begins with 'Forgiveness Sunday'; on the previous evening, after the office, in every family each member in turn bows down before the others, saying, 'Forgive me for the love of Christ'. The reply is, 'God forgive you and forgive me also'; and then they exchange an embrace. Each then repeats the same ceremony with his neighbours, friends and foes.

So, having started with what seemed like idolatry, we end up with something that has a touch of Jansenism. But in reality, the devout Russian worships God in spirit and truth; and body, sense and soul alike have their part in his worship.

Notes

1. *Russian Chronicle,* 1881, I, pp. 310–311.
2. In the story, *Following the Icon* (1887 and 1893).
3. The presence of the icons in similar circumstances was already recorded in tradition. On the 12th (N.S. 23rd) of January, 1772, the Cossacks of Yayik went in a body to request General Traubenberg to respect their liberties; and they too had the icons borne before them. The general ordered his men to fire on them. This was the prelude to

the great rebellion of Pugachev, just as the volleys fired in January 1905 were the preclude to the 1905 revolution.

4. At Kazan in 1837. Lerner, *Récits sur Pouchkine*, p. 171.
5. *Life of S.Seraphim of Sarov*, Murom, 1893, p. 147.
6. Fr Gratieux, in the *Revue du Clergé français* (15 August, 1911), published a penetrating study on *Les icônes et les Russes*. The Russian priest Chetverikov writes (*Optina Poustyne*, p. 88): 'I can confirm that the worship of icons by the Russian people is truly spiritual and Orthodox'. There is a chapter on 'Icons and their Veneration' in S. Bulgakov, *The Orthodox Church* (London, 1936).
7. *Spiritual Reading (Dushepoleznoe Chtenie)*, 1861, November, p. 306.
8. Zenzinov, *Encounter with Russia* (in Russian), New York, 1945, p. 373. On blessing at the point of death, see, for example, the *Autobiography* of the painter Maksimov, p. 149.
9. *Ethnographical Review (Etnograficheskoe Obozrenie)*, III (1889), pp. 44–45.
10. An expression resulting from a popular etymology: *malinovy*, which in fact describes the carillons 'of Malines', has been taken for the adjective derived from *malina*, 'raspberry'.
11. The Soviet writer Seifullina's novel *Virniea* (1924) is based on this custom.

3. THE VIRTUES

Relations with God

The Russian believer, as we have already seen, is not simply imbued with a diffused awareness of Providence. He believes with a solid faith, a faith which is rational without being the fruit of scholastic deduction. Indeed, he is conscious of the need to justify his faith, morally and even logically: the sects are witness to this need, which has led them to reject various aspects of their original belief; so are the religious disputes of which the public is so fond (I am thinking of the annual debates which used to be held at Lake Svetloiar,[1] and of the weekly meetings on the Spassky Esplanade in Moscow),[2] and the tormented theological questioning which we find here and there in histories and biographies, the struggle to understand the existence of evil, the Trinity, the resurrection of the dead and other mysteries.[3] This need is, very properly, allied to a deep respect for the essence of the mystery which it is not given to man to penetrate.

The Russian believer has no less strong a grasp of the other theological virtues, and before all else, he hopes in God alone. He has none of the fatuous confidence of Westernman—a Molinist *malgré lui*—who imagines that he can attain salvation by his own powers and his own will. No-one has so deep a sense of the weakness of his nature, the might of the devil, of man torn apart between good and evil; and, consequently, no-one has a so deep a sense of the necessity of grace. This divine succour he confidently expects, as he looks forward to the glory of Heaven—always provided his own evil will creates no obstacle. This confidence is expressed in many commonly-heard phrases; and it is this which explains the great catastrophies, when the devil has the upper hand, and the great conversions of which Russian literature furnishes so many examples.

In short, God, for the Russian, is a being very close to him, a being whom he can love as someone akin to himself; for he never forgets that man is made in God's image, after his likeness. In the person of Christ, God is—to an ideal degree, no doubt, but nonetheless very concretely—a dweller and a wanderer on the soil of Russia: you may encounter him any day. This feeling has been given rather naive expression by, for example, the poet Yesenin, a peasant of the Ryazan province; and Leskov himself wrote a story, *Christ comes to Call on the Peasant*.

This is the God who is believed in, hoped in, and loved, the same God who is adored. And how better to render such adoration than through the perfect conformity of one's own will to his, in conscious acceptance of the ordering of the world? If there is suffering, it must be borne without complaint, though it may seem to you to be unjust, excessive, or incomprehensible. The unbeliever Turgenev Finely depicts this typical Russian resignation to suffering in his story, *A Living Relic*, added to the later editions of *A Sportman's Sketches*. This resignation extends even to the acceptance of undeserved violent death, which is assimilated to the witness of the martyrs: the first saints of the Russian people were the young princes Boris and Gleb, who in 1015 fell to the assaults of the murderers sent by their elder brother Svyatopolk, without offering any resistance.

Natural death too must be welcome. 'By the judgement of God, he is no more' is a common formula. It seems to me that Tolstoy has somewhat distorted this ease in the presence of death by giving it a naturalistic colouring: in his view, the peasant dies almost as simply as does the tree . . . The peasant's death may be simple, certainly, but it is fully conscious: otherwise there would hardly be such prolonged preparations, the shift of coarse brown holland, the *lapti*, the coffin stored in the yard, the whole ritual. Death is simply accepted as part of the divine order, which is why you can speak quite naturally to an invalid or an old man about his approaching death.

Adoration includes prayer, prayer out of pure devotion, thanksgiving and also petitionary prayer. In 1844, Nikolai Shipov, a serf ill-treated by his master, whispered these words as he escaped from his village: 'Almighty God, inspire me, and give ear to the desire of my soul, if not for my sake, a least for my son's. Merciful Creator, give me endurance, patience to bear all misfortunes! And for the rest, they will be done!' He was taken prisoner by the mountaineers of the Caucasus, fled, lost his

26

way, and stopped to murmur under his breath: 'Saviour, bring thine unworthy servant hence! Let no enemies or wild beasts tear my body apart in this unclean land. Grant me to appear before thy holy sepulchre in Jerusalem, there to shed tears of gratitude!'⁴ And at the present time, in 1940, parents writing to their son, a soldier at the front in Finland, can say this: 'God grant you remain where you are! And may he give you good fortune and help you to keep alive till your return'.⁵

No empty formulae, these, but living prayer. It would be impossible to claim that the whole of the religious populace of Russia put into practice St Paul's injunction to 'pray without ceasing', but it is nonetheless a fact that the form of words which expresses this—the ejaculatory prayer, 'Lord Jesus Christ, Son of God, have mercy upon us!'—has nowhere been so universally employed. Inherited from the mystics of Athos, and circulated among the hermitages, it was in the seventeenth century 'the prayer' *par excellence.* Precisely because of its roots among the common people, it resisted the vague rationalism which overwhelmed the Church in the eighteenth century; apart from a slight variation, it united the 'Nikonians' and the Old Believers; and is still constantly on the lips of pious persons.⁶

Prayer involves not only the lips or the mind or the heart: it stirs the whole of one's being. Tears are never far away, pouring out spontaneously: they accompany all devout feelings—contemplation of God in the created world, contrition, compassion, charitable deeds. This is the virtue of tenderness, so dear to the simple soul.

God must not be offended. The Russians have a vivid sensitivity to sin: if someone does something that revolts you, the reproach you cast at him is 'You can't believe in God!'; and this phrase relates not so much to the punishment foreseen as to the injury done to the Holiness of God and of man who is his image. The word 'sin' crops up in many sayings where we should not expect it. Whenever we say, 'It is wicked to do so-and-so', 'It is not wicked to do so-and-so', 'As much good as harm', or 'What good is it to hide it?' the idea of sin is introduced. There is a proverb, 'Do not fear the knout, fear sin!' It does not by any means follow that sin is always avoided, but it is always recognised as such; and as a result the necessity for penitence is keenly felt, and the doctrine of redemption becomes a living reality. The heart of the people, so very sensitive to human misery, has always been forcibly struck by those

27

New Testament passages which say that where sin abounds grace abounds also, and that there is more joy in heaven over one repentant sinner than over ninety-nine righteous men who have no need of repentance. In *The Idiot*, when the peasant sees a child giving its first smile, his first thought is to cross himself, explaining, 'It's because God experiences the very same delight every time a sinner stands before him praying from the bottom of his heart'.[7]

Hence also come such familiar distortions as Korolenko puts into the mouth of his Siberian brigand, *The Assassin*, in the words: 'Real repentance is sweet . . . Only God is sinless, man's a sinner by nature and he saves himself by repentance . . . No sin, no repentance; and no repentance, no salvation'. This, according to their enemies, is exactly the teaching of the sectarians, the teaching which has also been attributed to Rasputin. No doubt, distortion to this extent is rare enough; but it is the natural issue of acute awareness of man's weakness and the power of penitence, as we see from many repeated instances during the last four centuries in the West. People are liable to sin, to let themselves fall into the toils of the devil because they hold the will do be of no account and because they are not aware of any marked difference between one sin and another. The Russians are not in the habit of drawing up catalogues, they do not make a gulf between mortal and venial sins; even the theologians make such a distinction only in imitation of the Western manuals. In the same chapter of *The Idiot*, a soldier sells his cross for money to drink, thoroughly defrauding the buyer; a peasant cold-bloodedly murders his friend—not because of any great need but out of sheer whim, because he has taken a fancy to his watch—after lifting his eyes to heaven and saying, 'Lord, forgive me, for the love of Christ!' Of course, this occurs in a novel; but Dostoyevsky invents nothing: these are random facts which he stores up as typical. Then comes repentance, a penitence as total as the sin. We are familiar with the figure of the businessman, ruthless to the point of inhumanity, who suddenly gives everything away and reduces himself to beggary—Gorky's *Foma Gordeev*, and plenty of others in real life. The reminiscences of the Missionary offer a wealth of instances of great crimes followed by wonderful reforms. In this way the 'absolute' character of the Russian people is reflected in the religious sphere. The modern Western believer, who has no end of trouble in believing that everything does *not* depend

28

on the right ordering of his will, knows nothing of such extreme cases of fall and restoration.

The Russians are no more eager to abdicate their freedom in their religion than in any other sphere. They are rebels against all precise and definite ordinances, more sensitive to the spirit than the letter. While they desire to give God the worship due to him, they do not see why attendance at Mass should be made an absolute obligation, as it is for the Latins. While they are capable of extraordinary asceticism, they still regard the observance of facts and Lenten abstinence as a private matter. With even stronger reason, they can hardly understand why the interpretation of a dogma should be defined, or the conduct of a believer condemned, by authority. There is conflict between the society of the faithful and the hierarchical Church precisely insofar as the latter claims the right to impose such condemnations, definitions or disciplinary measures. When rigorist clergy in the seventeenth century set out to enforce the regulations in all their strictness, the faithful wasted no time in expelling them with violence. The condemnations issued, through the ages, of apocryphal books, dubious entertainments, making the sign of the cross with two fingers, of fools for Christ's sake, wandering pilgrims, and unauthorised hermitages were never endorsed by popular feeling. Tolstoy had deliberately and publicly put himself outside the Church: but his excommunication was no less of a scandal for all that.

Relations with One's Neighbour

Everything we have so far said demonstrates how much the Russian people have been gripped by the Gospel: it is their book. It was an ancient custom in Voronezh for daughters to receive a copy of the Gospel as part of their dowry. When Gogol's future confessor, Father Matvei, was a young seminarian, he used to live at an inn where, every night, he went to read the Gospel to the carters: and these rough men listened with gratitude and emotion. Around 1895 the ex-convicts forcibly detained at Sakhalin asked their comrade, the 'political prisoner' L. Sternberg, to celebrate the Easter office for them—a great feast throughout Christendom, and there they were abandoned like animals!

He protested, 'But I am a Jew!' and they replied, 'That's all right, you know more about these things than any priest'. He accepted, and, during the night of the feast, he read to them the Gospel accounts of the Passion and Resurrection (which he knew by heart from former days) and the whole congregation broke into tears.[8] The Gospel is familiar from school, from various books in Slavonic or Russian, through preaching and through the extracts read at services. But it is summed up in the Beatitudes, sung by the choir every Sunday at the Liturgy: in these is the essence of Christianity, the divine paradox, in these the Russian people finds the sharp contrast which tears him away from this world and its miseries. When Peter the Great wished to destroy the ancient Russian devotions in his lust for material greatness, he ordered his creature Feofan Prokopovich to write on the Beatitudes—to make them harmless.

According to the *Spiritual Songs,* the sins most severely punished in Hell are sins against charity: theft, brigandage, murder, and also usury, slander and scandalmongering. In her introduction to *Ma vie,* Ch. Salomon relates how an *izvochnik* of Peterhof, shortly before the Revolution, confided to her: 'I think there is only one sin.' 'What is that?' 'To pass judgement on one's neighbour'.[9] There is a saying, 'Hell is built of hard hearts.' The worst accusations in day-to-day life are those of cruelty, covetousness, greed, injustice, and selfish calculation.

Man is never alone. He has brothers when he is not ashamed to call by that name—*brattsy, brat.* These brothers command no less respect than he does himself, and all alike are men. True enough, this or that category is, at certain times, excluded—non-Orthodox, non-Russians, 'enemies'; but this happens under the influence of political passions or government propaganda, and has nothing to do with the profoundly serious feeling for human community in every Russian soul.

There is thus in Russia a curiosity about all kinds of man, an interest in their lives, a sympathy with their sufferings, and an understanding of their opinions, even in religious matters. In the fifteenth century the Tver merchant, Afanasy Nikitin, could journey to the Indies harbouring not the least hostility towards Tartars and Muslims. In 1861, the rationalist writer Pryzhov, found himself in a village in the Moscow province during Great Lent, on Easter Eve in fact, and this at a time when the fast was regularly observed with great strictness; he ordered eggs, cheese and cream, and was served with these without any hint of criticism or comment.[10] Orthodox and Old Believers live harmoniously together: persecution comes only from the authorities. Our own Archimandrite Spiridon, the evangelist of Siberia, visited Hagia Sophia and stopped himself feeling any regret over the fact that it was then a mosque with the reflection that 'A mosque is also a temple of God'. This is most certainly not that cheap and hypocritical tolerance, based on misunderstanding or scepticism, which the century of Voltaire invented; it is a sincere respect for one's neighbour on the one hand, and for God on the other, God who alone searches the heart and knows his own.

The virtue most highly prized in the eyes of the people is that pity which is called *zhalost*. It is not a Russian peculiarity; we find it defined by St Isaac the Syrian as 'a heart on fire for the sake of all created things, men, birds, animals, devils, every creature. Remembering them and seeing them, the eyes shed tears, and the heart is melted by the great and ardent pity that possesses it, by great compassion. It cannot bear to hear or see any creature suffering the least harm or grief'. But this universal charity has been remarkably well understood by the Russians. The young Spiridon felt 'pity for the dead, pity for the living, for all men without distinction of nationality, religion, age or sex'. Chekhov was not given to flattering his *Muzhiks*, yet he is compelled to note this tenderness among them. Listening to the St Matthew's story of Herod looking for the new-born child to destroy him, Olga and Maria the sister of Ivan Makarych burst into tears, and all the neighbours are moved and pleased. The sceptical novelist treats this with irony, no doubt finding it ridiculous: but this only gives the more value to the account.

When it is not a question of one's brother far away, but of real and concrete neighbours, *zhalost* means in practice welcoming anyone who turns up, open and generous hospitality, satisfying needs, sharing sorrows, and giving to beggars, not in a distant and cold way, but with evangelical compassion. All the parables are constantly recalled—Dives and Lazarus, 'Blessed are the poor,' and the promised Judgement.

'Blessed are the meek'. Dostoyevsky, in *The House of the Dead*, notes that, on feast-days (days, that is, of great religious emotion), convicts, who are usually hard and brutal, leave off quarrelling and fighting and divide the alms given them from outside without any dispute; they become friendly and kind. 'It seemed that a sort of amity reigned among

31

them'. They exchange good wishes even with their warders.

The absence in Russia of what one may call the sense of honour has often been remarked and deplored. The duel did not exist until it was introduced with other Western fashions. People have found that, even among the upper classes, human dignity is ignored in Russia: for a long time, noblemen were liable to corporal punishment just as much as commoners were; no-one was ashamed of being seen drunk, or of living as a parasite. But the borderline between dignity and arrogance is by no means clear. Neither dignity as such, nor—still less—honour, is a virtue commended in the Gospel: it is not from this point of view that drunkenness or parasitism is culpable. The Russians have not forgotten that a wretched man of humble heart has more worth in the eyes of Christ than a righteous man who is proud or ambitious. They cannot readily understand the sentiment of *amour-propre*.

The desire to wield authority cannot be reconciled with this notion of Christianity. The Russian does not easily grasp the common and illusory excuse that one may desire to command one's fellows in order to serve them. On the contrary, what he delights in is humility. This is the characteristic which he delights to find in the clergy and admires in the saints. Vasili Rozanov, a writer who, for all his eccentricities, knew his people very well, said that every nation had its sacred ideal, expressing its best and highest virtue: and for Russia this virtue is humility. It conceals a very exalted beauty: 'It seems to enter into the essential composition of our idea of holiness'.[11]

Humility is so characteristic, so marked, and so consistent a feature of the Russian Christian that no other nation has taken so small a part in its own government. The Slavophils drew what were perhaps some rather extreme conclusions from this, but the fact remains no less certain. Under the old régime—as also since the Revolution—the proportion of non-Russians in positions of authority was always considerable, not at all because the Russians were intellectually less competent to fill them, but because for moral reasons they had no wish to do so. The Russians excel rather in a context of equality: in community, in cooperation, in assemblies of all sorts. And it is impossible not to see in this a result of their religious attitudes.

Humility must be practically demonstrated in external simplicity. The Russians love to watch the Liturgy in all its magnificence, but what they respect above all in their pastors is simplicity, in manners, in speech and in thought. They have never invented the pulpit, preferring to hear less clearly. And even the most splended of their ceremonies seem to us deficient in their lack of mere ceremonial. For much stronger reasons they demand in their human relationships a natural 'placid simplicity', as Leskov somewhere calls it.

Humility, the refusal to pass judgement, respect for others, pity are all, it may be said, very passive virtues; and some philosophers, Berdyaev, for instance, have drawn conclusions from this about the essential feminity of the Russian people. However, there is one idea which the Russians have made into an exceptional case, the idea of the 'exploit', the *podvig*. It is a *podvig* every time you choose the more difficult way, every time you triumph over yourself to whatever degree and in whatever manner. The *podvig* is Christian heroism, beginning with conscientious performance of the simplest duties, developing through asceticism, and culminating in total sacrifice. 'Greater love hath no man than this, that a man lay down his life for his friends'. This too is practised in Russia. A child's nurse, seventy years old, to save the infant she was looking after from a carriage rushing headlong towards them, leapt back and lay on top of the child, so that it was her body that was crushed and trampled by the horses.[12] This, of course, is not typically and exclusively Russian. What is more definitely so is the sense that the Gospel is there to be put into practice. More than most peoples the Russians are scandalised by disparity between teaching and conduct. They are not happy to allow any distinction between percepts and counsels, regarding it as a mere quibble.

Here is the case of a young boy belonging to the merchant class—people of the type we have spoken of as morally unstable, capable of the best and the worst behaviour—a boy taught according to the ethic of the Sermon on the Mount. For a long time he fights back: in particular he is harsh towards the poor; but at last he is converted. One day, when one of his schoolfellows, coming from a very poor background, is about to be sent home from school for not being properly dressed, he gives him his own uniform. His friends are full of admiration. But when he goes home he is beaten. His nanny understands and defends him, and she is shown the door. The bewildered child pours out his feelings to the chaplain: 'Christ said . . .' The other retorts, 'Obey

33

your parents, ask their pardon, and don't do it again'. From that day on he becomes pensive, stops working, and wanders around like a lost soul, asking everyone, 'I did what they taught me to do and they beat me: why?' One morning he goes out for a bathe and does not come back; they decide that he must have fallen down the steepest part of the bank. But at the funeral his nanny bows down to the ground before his body and says, 'The sin is upon his parents. He drowned himself on purpose, because he could not bear this contradiction: they taught him one thing but treated him otherwise. They spoke like God and acted like Satan. His wits were turned and his soul was sickened by it'.[13]

This child and his nanny speak for the Russian people when confronted by the State and its institutions. The Bible says, 'Thou shalt not kill', and the State puts men to death and sends men to war. The Gospel's teaching is 'Judge not . . . Love one another . . . Turn the other cheek . . . Woe to the rich!' and the State holds assizes, throws men into prison, and defends the rich against the poor. Other people under other skies accept these contradictions with a light heart; but the Russians have taken Christian teaching seriously. They know that the kingdom of God is not of this world, but they know too that even on earth a 'kingdom' of sorts must be constructed, justice and truth must be practised, and it is this righteousness, this *pravda*, that they thirst for. When it is only their own persons that are involved they are meek, humble and submissive; but where their brothers are concerned, where the social community is concerned, they become capable of rebellion, capable of reclaiming their rights, denying and rejecting and destroying overnight all that stand in the way of the realisation of their religious ideal.

Hence come the countless 'seekers after righteousness' (*pravdoisakateli*) among the people, who so astonish the modern West: those who devote themselves in all simplicity to their calling, those who are literally sickened by injustice, who abandon the world of Antichrist and take to the roads, roaming as far as the strange and inaccessible land of the White Waters[14] in their search for the perfect Church. They defy the law and its officers to serve mankind, and strive to create a modern Christianity out of the Revolution: millions of them believed in 1917 that a world without war and oppression had been established . . . This side of Russian religion, characterised by some as antisocial, anarchic and utopian, nevertheless arises naturally from the reception of Gospel and Bible by sincere hearts; it is very typical and well worthy of note.

It is shown in its most charitable form in the popular attitude towards condemned criminals. For the positivist or the nominal Christian, these are simply criminals and so are no longer human beings; for the Russian people, Christians without any superstitious respect for social institutions, a condemned man is not necessarily a guilty man, and a crime is not an absolute and definite evil so much as a sin requiring pardon, however great the crime may be. 'The assassin himself does not spend all his time killing, he lives his life and feels what other men feel', says Korolenko after a long experience of prisons and transit-camps.[15] The sympathy of the simple folk for the 'unfortunate'—the condemned criminals—is no legend but a reality proven a hundred times over. In Siberia, where the people are tough, Dostoyevsky says that 'there was not one merchant, not one worthy of the town, who did not send something' to the convicts at Christmas. Pots of *kasha* and even felt boots are left on windowsills for runaway convicts. In Moscow the merchants go on foot from their central quarter, Trans-Moskva, to the furthest boundary at Rogozha to give alms to the prisoners leaving to be deported. At Easter, well-to-do families cook eggs and cakes for the prisoners.

In 1866, a certain Sergeant Shibunin was arrested for striking his commanding officer; the peasants constantly bought him gifts: one would bring a jug of milk, another some rye-biscuits or eggs, another some pieces of cloth. When he went before the firing-squad, the crowd fell on their knees, intoning prayers. Candles and coins were thrown on his grave, and the office of the Dead was celebrated there until the Police Commissioner put it out of bounds. Twelve years later, E. M. Vogüé visited Orel and saw three thieves in the pillory in the main square, condemened by the court to the mockery of the public; but the public lavished food and money on them. In Petersburg in 1915, Maurice Paléologue, the French Ambassador, came across four soldiers leading some poor soul, handcuffed and submissive, off to jail: suddenly a local woman came up and gave a small coin to the captive, crossing herself as she did so, and the soldiers 'slowed their pace and moved apart to let her go through to do it'.[17] During the 1914 war, the peasants would bring out food and drink for the German and Austrian prisoners of war whenever the trains halted.

As far as the Christian peasant is concerned, the State, with its courts and its punitive cruelties, is only a relative authority compared with the force of the Gospel's teachings. He does not blame the State at all, since it is the order willed—or tolerated—by God; but, for his own part, he would rather not bother with it: he will act according to his duty as a Christian.

The order willed by God? How is this possible? The contradiction between the State and the Gospel is surely too great. Regrettably, however, Church and State are bound up together, as one observes all too frequently. So, in the moral as in the dogmatic sphere, scandal, doubt, and questioning are generated, and sects are born. Hence the success of, for example, the Dukhobors and the Tolstoyans, of evangelistic preachers, pilgrims, 'abstinents', and many others, who refuse to pay taxes, to accept military service or take civic office.

It should never be forgotten that, for the soldiers and peasants who created it, the 1917 Revolution was a movement of Christian protest against the State. It was a revolt against war, an absurd and un-justifiable war, a revolt in the name of this motto—itself a liturgical phrase—which from the first day on was painted on the banners of the Revolution's Christian inspiration which gave it such universal injustice in the name of the motto, drawn from St Paul, confirmed in the first Soviet Constitution: 'If a man will not work, neither let him eat!' It was a revolt against artificial inequality, class distinctions, and hollow titles in the name of the Christian motto of brotherhood. It was the Revolution's Christian inspiration which gave it such universal appeal.[18] The priests supported it, and the landlords resigned themselves to it, not being fully convinced that their claims to their property were well-founded. Who then were its opponents? They were found among the circles permeated by Western ideas, among those who worshipped the State, the Nation or the Law, and had little concern for Christianity—in short, the intellectuals and the 'cadet' party surroun-ding them, and the professional servants of the régime, higher dignitaries, officers, police authorities. Popular unanimity was broken only to the extent that the Christian inspiration of the Revolution was replaced by the growing influence of parties appealing to quite different doctines and looking to very different ends.

Thus the evangelical Christianity of the Russian people extends into the social and political sphere; at the right moment, it can take forms which are not passive but literally explosive. What is manifested in 1917 is the ancient cosmic and apocalyptic basis of Russian religion, the longing to create a new world. After this, its other aspects, humility and acceptance, reasserted themselves. How is it that this devout nation could permit the closing and destruction of its churches, the profanation of its icons and relics, the arrest and execution of its clergy? There was occasional resistance, but, on the whole, the people yielded to pressure: 'Give place to the wrath of God' said St Paul. Everything was permitted, everything was yielded. They appeared to have abaonded their faith.[19] But they preserved it beneath their silence and external submission: wandering priests in disguise, secret monastic professions, collective baptisms, delayed general absolutions over earth brought from graves, and many other ingenious expedients. Martyrdom was accepted when necessary but not eagerly sought. In this way, active and passive virtues give place to each other and combine with each other. The religion of the Russian people is by no means a simple, paltry, throughtless affair.

Notes

1. A lake in the forests of the Vetluga, in whose depths men of pure life used to see the city of Kitezh, which miraculously vanished into the waters at the approach of the Tartars. Each year, on 22 June (O.S.), Orthodox, Old Believers and sectarians would meet there to discuss their faith. These debates have been described by Merezhkovsky and Prishvin, and were observed by Korolenko.
2. Mentioned by Haxthausen in his *Studies on the Interior Situation of Russia:* I have also witnessed these myself.
3. Of such sort are the tempestuous debates between Archpriest Avvakum and the deacon Fyodor, in their prison at Pustozersk in the seventeenth century.
4. N. Shipov, *The Story of My Life*, Moscow, 1933, pp. 448–449, 493.
5. Zenzinov, *op. cit.*, p. 242.
6. On the prayer of Jesus, Mme Behr-Sigel's article (*Dieu Vivant*, no. 8, pp. 69–84) is obligatory reading, as is also of course, 'The Way of a Pilgrim', which illustrates the custom.

7. Dostoyevsky, *The Idiot*, Part II, ch. 4.

8. *Korolenko* (an anthology), Petrograd, 1922, pp. 64–65.

9. Ch. Salomon, *Ma vie, Récit d'une paysanne russe*, revised and corrected by Leo Tolstoy, Paris, 1923, pp. 21–22.

10. Pryzhov, *Sketches, Articles and Letters*, Moscow, 1934, p. 226.

11. Rozanov, *The Siberian Wanderer* (Rasputin), in *An Apocalyptic Sect*, St Petersburg, 1914, p. 204.

12. V. Karpov, *Memories*, 1933, p. 32.

13. *Ibid.*, pp. 25–31.

14. See my *Avvakum et les débuts du raskol*, Paris, 1938 (2nd ed., 1963), pp. 656–566.

15. *Korolenko* (an anthology), Petrograd, 1922, p. 63.

16. Biryukov, *Leo Tolstoy, a Biography* II, p. 104.

17. M. Paléologue, *La Russie des Tsars*, I, p. 283.

18. Many revolutionaries—terrorists even—were Christians: Sazonov, who murdered the minister Plehve in 1904, was an Old Believer, inspired by the love of humanity. 'Everything is simple for the man who lives with 'God', he wrote; and his own life was that of a saint. The journalist Ludovic Naudeau (*Les dessous du chaos russe*, Paris, 1920, p. 89) recalls how, when he was in prison with the revolutionary socialists under the Bolshevik régime, 'Many of these rough souls, veterans of the struggles against Tsarism, used every night to fall on their knees . . . crossing themselves fervently and praying'.

19. Gorky was amazed—and triumphant—at this lack of reaction (*On the Russian Peasant*, Berlin, 1922, pp. 29–30).

4. THE HIGHER TYPES OF DEVOTION

So far, we have been observing the religion of the common man; but the Russians are familiar with a higher level of religion. They experience a thirst for heroism from time to time, and voluntarily give themselves to asceticism. It is a good thing to accept suffering: heroism consists in *provoking* it. Dostoyevsky has strongly emphasised the redemptive value which simple Christians attribute to voluntary suffering. One may read, in the *House of the Dead*, the story of a gentle and docile convict, a great reader of the Bible, who suddenly refuses to work. When the Commandant come by, he throws a brick at him, as if he wanted to hit him hard. He is flogged to death, but protests in his last agony that he never wanted to kill, only to 'suffer'. His memory was preserved in the camp with respect.[1] Voluntarily to risk death is to imitate Christ.

A more frequent instance of the religious 'exploit' is provided by pilgrimages[2]—not, in this case, comfortable and swift journeys by rail, or, these days, by air, organised in advance by agencies. If a peasant, male or female, whatever his or her age, one day feels the need to leave behind earthly ties, duties, cares and loves, to set free his soul, they go off, on foot of course, with stick and knapsack, in the direction of whatever holy places they know. Perhaps there will be a hermitage nearby where a revered ascetic lives, a man who can read other men's hearts and offer counsel and consolation—a *starets,* as they say. Our pilgrim will stay a while there and return, a new man, to his home. Or perhaps he will carry on, touring all the hermitages in the district. Sometimes, however, his liberation extends over a period of months: he may go to Suzdal, Great Rostov, St Sergei, Sarov, Valaam, the Solovki islands in the White Sea; to the sanctuaries of Great Novgorod, Moscow, or Voronezh; or to the south, to the Lavra at Kiev, where, along galleries hewn out of the rock, the bodies of holy men lie sleeping in their hundreds. It was here, in the churches, the refectory, and the courts and terraces overlooking the Dnieper, that one used to see

39

myriads of men and women, old and young, flowing in ceaselessly from all corners of Russia, freed from the servitude of daily life, in their long kaftans and home-woven leggings: some would be absorbed in prayer, others would be enjoying the divine beauty of the site, or, perhaps, would be earning their living singing *Lazarus*, or *Alexei the man of God*, or other 'spiritual songs'. Nothing could have been more moving than such a great concentration of Russian popular piety; nothing could better have evoked what the great pilgrimages of the West must have been like.

But for those who went on pilgrimages there remained a more distant and difficult ideal: to go to the sanctuaries of Tsargrad (Constantinople), to Mount Athos and to Palestine, to holy places *par excellence* which are constantly mentioned in the Gospel and the Saints' Lives. For this they must organise themselves in groups, take ship, and put up with a hard journey and the risk of sickness, always in absolute poverty. Vogüé admiringly observed these Russian pilgrims, animated by 'a flame of authentic and immense faith'; and he adds, 'Many do not believe that they have completed their pilgrimage when they get to Jerusalem, but press on through the fatigue and misery of several months' trudging through the Arabian deserts to kiss the rocks that Moses touched'.[3] Here is a *podvig* towards which one might well aspire all one's life and after which one might die; yet these *podvizhniki*, these heroes, were numbered not in dozens but in thousands each year. There was sometimes a kind of epidemic of departures: twice—around 1830 and 1850—numbers of youths, sons of merchants, fifteen or sixteen years old, left for Mount Athos from Stary-Oskol in the Kursk Province; many stayed on Athos and took the habit.

The memoirs of the Missionary, like the *Way of a Pilgrim*, testify to the considerable place which pilgrimages occupied in Russian piety. We can say that this type of devotion was accepted and practised even among the upper classes: at the beginning of the ninteteenth century many of the gentry 'used to spend the summer travelling from one monastery to another',[4] and the learned philologist Nevostruev would go every year from Moscow to the Troitsa-Sergei Monastery on foot with sack and staff.[5]

Not all had either the possibility or the desire to leave their families, their property, and their comfort to march along the roads of Holy

Russia; but at least they feel admiration and respect for those who have the courage to do so. When Gogol and his friend Maximovich were going towards the renowned hermitage of Optina Pustyn, they wanted to buy a punnet of strawberries from a young peasant girl who was taking them to sell in the market; but she gave it to them, saying, 'How could I take money from pilgrims?'

If it is a first step in spiritual maturity to leave one's home, is it not better still to make pilgrimage a permanent state? It is for this reason that there exists a higher devotional type, the state of the wanderer, the *strannik*, perfectly exemplified by the *Way of a Pilgrim*.[6] The wanderer has often been led to adopt this way of life by special circumstances: a natural or accidental infirmity may have made him unfit for strenuous work; an event such as the death of a wife, a fire, or an imperative vision may have detached him from his wordly goods. No more is needed for his meditative spirit and religious soul to set him on his way. As the sum total of his possessions, he takes a long garment, a hat, a wallet with some crusts in it, and sets off. Like those we have already seen, he goes on pigrimage from monastery to monastery; but in his case it is prolonged indefinitely with no plans for returning. He is hospitably received everywhere: in return he does some menial duty,—or perhaps simply talks, recounting his edifying memories, describing the wonders of the holy places, the exploits of the ascetics, and so giving his hosts food for thought, lifting them out of their earthbound daily life. If he can read, he may read to them from the Gospel, the Desert Fathers or the Lives of the Saints. For his hearers it is a veritable feast, a wonder, and a life-giving memory for a long time afterwards. Thousands of these wanderers travelled the length and breadth of Russia. Fr Matvei at Kiev would receive sometimes up to forty of them each day. Tolstoy knew and loved them, Bunin described them, Chaliapin used to mingle with them. The peasant poet Yesenin recalls how his grandmother's house was always full of wanderers, men and women, and invalids, who would sing legendary tales and laments as they passed through the little towns.[7]

Such was the great religious role played by the wanders. The people's generosity towards them encouraged some abuses, and there was no lack of impostors, wanderers whose only 'vocation' was idleness or vagrancy. These are no concern of ours; but they provided the positivistically-minded and the authorities with a pretext for persecuting and denigrating this devotion as such.

A life without hearth or home did not totally satisfy the appetite for perfection; that required further refinements of its own. Some wished to make up what was lacking by special austerities. They would go on their way hung about with weights, stones in their knapsacks, or even chains all over their bodies. Early Christianity, in Syria, had its 'siderophoroi', 'iron-bearers': Russian piety did not fail to provide similar instances. E. M. de Vogüé saw in Jerusalem 'a huge cross of crude iron, weighing eighteen or twenty pounds. . . which was discovered hung around the neck of an old woman who died in the hospice [the Russian Hospice in Jerusalem]: this poor woman had come on foot from Jaffa with this strange variation on the hair-shirt which she had worn for years'. These pieces of iron are called *verigi*.

Let us follow the ideal of *podvig* a little further. In Syria, the homeland of all religious excesses, the Christians of the first few centuries took quite literally the Apostle's words, 'The foolishness of God is wiser than the wisdom of men . . . we are fools for Christ's sake', and the idiot, the *salos,* became a familiar sight. What more meritorious exploit could there be than to renounce man's peculiar property, his pride and joy, the reason itself, and pass oneself off as mad, so as to invite as many indignities as possible, to fall to the lowest point of abjection, willingly, for the love of Christ? As soon as they were converted, the Russians were seized by the desire to emulate such behaviour: there were voluntary idiots at Kiev from the eleventh century onwards, the *yurodivy*. And they did not die out but continued to exist through the Muscovite period and later, resisting harassment by civic authorities, condemnation by enlightened eighteenth century prelates, indignant scorn from intellectual circles and Soviet 'cultural' propaganda. They still exist today. These too wander around with *verigi* and iron hats, absurdly dressed in rags or half-naked, begging, rolling in the dirt, inviting jeers and blows with their offensive words and grotesque or objectionable acts. They have put to death their feelings of sensitivity and self-respect; they are a scandal, respecting nothing, like beings from another world. They are despised and they are admired. Their exceptional qualities are recognised—they read men's hearts and see into the future. Their least word is interpreted as significant, and sometimes they have also played a part in politics, castigating those in power. Ivan the Terrible could have a metropolitan put to death, but he put up with the invective of a *yurodivy*.[8] At the present day, they are directors of conscience for the people. The *yurodivy* is ubiquitous. It was a *yurodivy* of Kursk who was to be the future St Serafim of Sarov. Another, a pilgrim to Palestine who had become a monk, founded the Gethsemane hermitage near the monastery of St Sergei. A priest of Uglich named Pyotr who had the reputation of a *yurodivy* (he was spoken of as mad, suspended and even chained up in his house) was, for forty years before his death in 1866, visited by crowds eager for his advice and was regarded as a spiritual director by many scholars and philosophers, including the archimandrite and professor Fyodor (Bukharev). There is no lack of writers to describe the *yurodivy*, with greater or lesser intelligence and sympathy: Tolstoy, in his *Childhood*, Dostoyevsky, in *The Possessed*, the satirist Saltykov-Shchedrin, the journalists Gleb Uspensky and Naumov; Pryzhov and Korolenko have devoted studies to them. In no case does anyone question that this is an eminently representative manifestation of Russian popular piety at its heroic level.[9]

All across Russia in the old days were a great number of hermitages, 'wildernesses' or *pustyn*, monastic establishments, certainly, but bearing only a very faint resemblance to the great monasteries equipped with large numbers of clergy, organised in full hierarchical order, with libraries, maintaining relations with the world outside, and frequented by civic and ecclesiastical dignitaries. The hermitages, in contrast, belonged to the people: they were located near peasant communities. Their life alternated work on the land, wood-cutting, and fishing with the offices; and these latter could hardly be very elaborate, since it was often hard to obtain the services of the indispensable priest and deacon. The peasant could withdraw to such places without ceasing to feel at home, in order to draw on the teaching available there, and the peace which his soul needed; his children would find teachers and guides there, reliable and familiar; and, finally, young or old could take the habit there, bringing only their strong arms and their good will.

If there was in such a community an exceptional monk, one who had been lucky enough to visit Mount Athos, or to sit at the feet of some great spiritual director, the hermitage would become a place of santification, a school of mystical prayer, for the whole region. He would not need to be a priest, certainly not a scholar or a great theologian; no more would he be the superior of the hermitage. His superiority would be a superiority of virtue, in particular that tender charity so dear to the hearts of the people, a sympathy leading to wonderful perceptiveness, experience of how different souls would relate to the conditions of their daily life and work, which in each individual case would suggest the best solution, simplicity of spirit, manners and speech, which would put the hublest visitor at his ease, and, at the same time, a natural authority, inspiring confidence and commanding obedience. His brothers in religion would come to him and reveal their most secret thoughts, according to the ancient precept about 'opening one's heart'; the peasants of the neighbourhood and the workmen and shopkeepers of the town would come and candidly confess to him even their material worries, as well as their pangs of conscience and their doubts, so as to receive his blessing and hear his opinion. Such was the *starets*, a man of the people who had attained the highest degree of wisdom complemented by divine grace, but one who still dwelt among the people, both in his inmost nature and in his actions. Official authorities, abbots and bishops, were often suspicious of the *starets*—he belonged to the people's religion, at once one of its highest manifestations and one of its wellsprings and luminaries.[10] Beside such very clearly marked types as the wanderers, the fools for the love of Christ, and the *startsy*, the picture we have of other types is much less distinct—the 'silent ones', *molchalniki*, the anchorites, *pustynniki*, the recluses, *zatvorniki*, and 'questers', *prochaki*. The last named devote themselves to travelling around Russia to collect the money necessary for the building of a church: sometimes they are expiating some great sin in this way, like Nekrasov's Vlas.[11] They must carry a register, given by the episcopal chancery, in which gifts are entered, and must be duly authorised by their own village community. Despite this, they are not always on the best of terms with the powers that be, and are no strangers to abuse and imprisonment. However this exploit is nothing compared with those we have already listed.

Another thing is that these lesser exploits are often temporary. The sort of person who undertakes them may be a man with frustrated expectations who fears that he will not be able to master his resentment and so takes a vow of absolute silence; in practice he may survive seven years without a word, and then begin to talk again.

The same individual often passes from one of these forms of life to another. At the beginning of the last century a respectable citizen of Kursk left everything, exchanged his clothes for those of a beggar whom he met, and became a *strannik*. One day he turned up at Kozelsk, in the Kaluga province, and without a word, took up employment as the priest's servant: he carried water, chopped wood, swept the yard and answered questions only by signs. Here he acts as a *molchalnik*. He was given alms at the church, in money and in kind, all of which he gave away to the poor, making do for himself with a bread roll: the town thanked Providence for giving them a saint. He spoke no more until the day of his death, and then only to make his confession.[12] Or again, some devout believer, wearied with the world, settles in the forest, makes himself a log cabin and lives there as an anchorite: this sometimes happens near a monastery, but the hermit does not depend on it and follows his own rule, as his fancy takes him—which is the reason for the authorities' complaints about hermits. Soon he will be well-known in the neighbourhood—a new saint, perhaps! People visit him, and he refuses to see them; or perhaps he does receive them and so himself becomes a spiritual director. After a while he disappears to become a 'wanderer'. Even among monks living under rule, stability is not regarded as a virtue: it appears only at the end of their lives. The most revered monks, those whose biographies are there for us to read, were 'gyrovagues' for decades—two years in this hermitage, five years in that, and so on.

Serafim of Sarov is a canonised saint (canonised, in fact, in 1903) whose life provides an admirable 'synopsis' of popular piety. He came of merchant stock in Kursk, and while still very young, developed a great love for the Liturgy and read the Bible and the Lives of the Saints. When he was eighteen, he set out on a pilgrimage to Kiev, where he visited the recluse Dosifei who had a reputation as a *starets*. Dosifei recommended him to practise perpetual prayer in the usual form—'Lord Jesus Christ, Son of God, have mercy on us!'—and sent him to the hermitage of Sarov in the Tambov province. He went there immediately and was professed after a few years. As soon as he was ordained priest, in the winter of 1794, he left the monastery and retired to

45

a hut two hours' walk away, with a copy of the Gospel and the indispensable sacred vessels; and there he lived as a solitary, dressed in a white tunic and breeches, *lapti* woven of bark on his feet, like a peasant, with a twenty pound iron cross on his breast and eight pounds more on his back, as well as a girdle of iron, never leaving his hut without carrying a bag of stones. He sang the psalms, read the ascetic Fathers, prayed and fasted. It was at this time that he was attacked by three brigands, and refrained from offering them the least resistance. From 1802 to 1805 our *pustynnik* becomes a *molchalnik*—no more visits, absolute silence—after which he returned to a normal regular life inside the monastery enclosure. On the 9 May 1810, he shut himself in his cells, opening the door to no-one, not even to the diocesan bishop; from then on he slept in his coffin, receiving communion through the window on Sundays and feast-days: he becomes a recluse, *zatvornik*. On the 25 November 1825, he left his enclosure and returned to his remote hut: but now that he had attained supreme wisdom, he was ready to play the role of *starets* until his death in 1833. He healed souls and bodies alike: under his influence, noblemen freed their serfs, monasteries were founded, the Spirit was released. What he taught, by word and example, was nothing more nor less than the religion we have tried to describe: gentleness, humility, pity and love; in general, the freedom of the soul with regard to the passions, to earthly concerns and to the mighty of this world. He worked miracles, foretold the future, discerned men's secret thoughts, and had mysterious relationships with other *startsi* like himself—Timon of Krivoogero, Daniel of Achinsk in Siberia and Yuri of Zadonsk.

The Spirit breathed around him in his lifetime, and has continued to do so right up to the present day; because in Serafim of Sarov the Russians recognised the high point of their religion. In him were combined the priest (but without any of the seminary theology which wavered between a decadent scholasticism borrowed from abroad and the corrosive philosphy of the Protestant schools), the monk (but without the formalities and limitations of a rule), the mystic (but without any merely bookish study of the hesychast writers, and without any ignorance of this world), and the layman, the simple believer—*prostolyudin*, as they say in Russian (but without his disastrous lapses from grace). This fusion and transcendence of professional

46

barriers, this essential freedom, is what the Russians love, in religion as elsewhere.[13]

Notes

1. *Notes from the House of the Dead*, I, 2. Similarly, in *Crime and Punishment*, V, 2, the young Nikolai has just accused himself of the moneylender's murder, in which he is not involved at all. Porfiry, the police magistrate, is not bothered by this false confession, because he knows the feelings of his people.
2. I have dealt at greater length with 'pilgrimages in Orthodoxy' in *Lumen Vitae*, vol. XIII (1958), no. 2, pp. 258–266.
3. E. M. de Vogüé, *Syrie, Palestine, Mont Athos*, Paris, 1876, pp. 212–214. A. Vasiliev, the Byzantinist, also relates his encounter with a group of eleven pilgrims at Sinai (*A Journey to Sinai*, St Petersburg, 1904, pp. 54–56).
4. Pumen, *Memories,* p. 328, in *Lectures Given to the Society for Russian History and the Antiquities at the University of Moscow*, 1877, vol. I.
5. *Christian Readings*, November 1914.
6. *Stories of a Strannik* in Russian: Western European languages have no corresponding technical term.
7. In his *Autobiography*.
8. Indications of their great role in the seventeenth century may be found in my *Avvakum et les débuts du raskol,* pp. 318–320 and *passim.*
9. *The yurodivy* has provided material for several studies in the West: Fr Lev (Gillet) in *Irénikon*, 1927, no 1, pp. 14–19; Hilpisch in *Zeitschrift fur Aszetik und Mystik*, vol. V (1931), pp. 121–131; Benz, in *Kyrios*, 1938, pp. 1–55; and, most notably, Gamayoun, in *Russie et Chrétienté*, 1938–39, no. 1, pp. 57–77. This last article is by far the best.
10. The *starets* type has been studied in the West by I. Smolitsch in *Leben und Lehre der Starzen*, Vienna, 1936 (2nd ed., Cologne, n.d.), and in several articles in the periodical *Kyrios*. I have dealt here only with its more popular side.
11. In the poem, *Who Can Live Well in Russia?*

12. *Discourses for the Home,* 1861, pp. 698–700.
13. There are some interesting reflections on the types we have been studying in Fr Tyszkiewicz's article, *Spiritualité et sainteté russe pravoslave,* in *Gregorianum,* XV (1934), pp. 349–376. For an account of St Serafim in French, see E. Behr—Sigel, *Prière et sainteté dans l'eglise russe,* Paris, 1950. pp. 108–120.

5. CONCLUSION

The 'Saints' and the People

Are these higher manifestations of popular piety, the various particular types we have described, 'external' to their setting and without influence on it? From what we have seen so far, we can already predict that this will not prove to be so. First of all, the *startsi*, the recluses, solitaries and wanderers, exceptional though they may be, are not rare. They exist everywhere, they crop up in every period and still flourish today, even after revolution, collectivisation and persecution. Everyone has come across them, everyone may discover them in his own neighbourhood. Next, the Russians do not see such a gulf existing between layman and priest, secular and monk, sinner and saint, and so do not regard these people as beings apart, to be admired from a distance. On the contrary, they belong to the people, who treat them with honour, are eager to meet them, love to associate with them, to be illuminated by their light and warmed by their fervour, and to relax in their company. The cells of even the most obscure persons of great piety are never empty of visitors, even when the general run of monks are regarded with a certain scepticism. Any sick or infirm person who is noted for patience beyond the common measure becomes an object of pilgrimage, a model, an oracle, and an inspirer of vocations.

Father Fyodor had a fall when he was very young, which left him paralysed in both legs: his mother promptly took him to visit a woman who had been bedridden for forty years, crippled in all four limbs, to whom the whole district would come for advice. She told the mother to buy a handful of candles on the Sunday following, to light them one by one in front of each of the icons, and to sing a *moleben* to the saint who received the last of them. The child recovered. When he was seventeen, a storm drove him one evening to knock on the window of an *izba*: he heard a voice saying, 'Come in, come in, I've been waiting for you for a

49

long time'. Without realising it, he had happened upon the same woman. He stayed with her for six years, looking after her and attending to her needs, while she expounded the Bible and the Gospel to him. At last she sent him to the monastery of Valaam, predicting that he would be driven away, but would return there—all of which came to pass. Father Fyodor was still alive in 1938.[1] Thus it is by means of these superior examples, who, nevertheless, still belong to the people, that the people's religion is constantly purified, elevated, and spiritualised.

The enthusiasm for sanctity is not without awkward consequences. All these superior manifestations have their antitypes—false *yurodivy*, false pilgrims and hermits, who may for a while abuse the generosity of the people. Or else it may happen that some who begin as genuine candidates for holiness are corrupted by this same generosity. One might ask what in reality was happening among the crowd of three hundred 'fools for Christ', wanderers, male and female, cripples and beggars, who in 1882 swept through towns and monasteries on their way to Kiev, under the leadership of Mother Matriona and at her expense, begging, clowning, singing, shouting, and feasting, but praying as well, and listening to readings from Scripture. The atheist writer Pryzhov joined the band disguised as a pilgrim, and it was after this experience that he wrote his (very unfair) book, *Twenty-Six Fools for Christ*.

Or again: it is enough if someone *shows* himself to be the equal of the saints. If you admire him, you do not ask him for guarantees of his orthodoxy; and so sects or quasi-sects are born—with the loose discipline of the Russian Church the distinction is sometimes rather fluid. In Rakovki, in the Samara province, 'Aunt Kuzminichna' organised a group of believers who read the Bible and sang 'canons'; certain missionaries suspected her of being affiliated to the *khlysty* sect, but the bishop, Gury, acquitted her of the charge. On the eve of the Revolution little churches were constantly springing up here and there, groups of anchoresses (*chernichki*), fasters (*postniki*), almsgivers or 'stephanians', abstinents, 'brothers in Christ', singers of akathists and sayers of prayer, all of whom, grouped around some venerated zealot, devoted themselves to some pious work or other; though this did not make them any less liable to isolate themselves from the Great Church and its clergy and to come closer to the actual sects defined and condemned by the Church.[2]

The Russians regard anathemas very lightly. Two Rumanian Origenists landed at a Russian town in the Crimea one day in 1872: at once, everbody left their work to come and hear them, and after a few weeks there were about a hundred *skoptsy* in the district.[3] This dreadful sect had been cursed by the Church, and its adherents were liable to be sent to the Siberian camps; but what should this matter if you believed you were obeying a verse of the Gospel?[4] All these facts provide, by their very absurdity, a confirmation of what we have said about the characteristics of popular religion.

The 'Saints' and the Upper Classes

It was often the higher instances of the people's piety that brought back to religion those social groups educated in the Western manner. A landowner of noble birth, a teacher at the high school in Orel, who ridiculed the credulity of the peasants as a matter of course, was converted by a *yurodivy* whom he met at his sister's home. Think of what must have been done to nourish, develop or illustrate Christian feelings among the children of the squirearchy by *stranniks* entertained in the servants' hall. A nobleman, a general or a student, on pilgrimage to the St Sergi Monastery or the Caves at Kiev, might happen to be present when a *starets* was receiving the faithful; and he might be moved to wonder whether, in this naïve faith and trust of the simple people, there was not perhaps something other than ignorance and supersitition. The *Lives* of the great *startsi* are full of incidents of this sort: we have here one of the points of contact between the religion of the people, which we have attempted to study in isolation, and Russian religion in general.

More to this, however. Peter the Great's reform consisted in the creation in Russia of a governing class educated in the European manner, and as totally removed from belief as from the national costume, which had equally been declared barbaric. Now in Europe this was the time of the 'philosophy of enlightenment'—a proud confidence in human reason and infinite progress, the rejection of all values not purely rational, contempt for the Church and hatred for all the clergy. Voltaire had innumerable followers in cultivated circles in Russia. In short, the intellectual world utterly rejected Orthodoxy, and the official world saw in it no more than a pattern of decent behaviour and a pastime for the common

51

people; those most committed to Christianity, the higher ranks of the clergy, for example, retained a bare senstivity to ethical matters and no more. By the close of the eighteenth century, dechristianisation was complete, and when dissatifaction with rationalism set in, it was to Freemasony or Martinism that people turned, not to Orthodoxy. But, providentially, Orthodoxy lived on among the common people; and it was the common people who, directly or indirectly, produced the revival of Orthodoxy among the intelligentsia.

It occurred directly in the case of Sergei Soloviev, the famous historian, a priest's son, but heavily influenced by fashionable positivism. Three times in her life, his old nurse had gone on pilgrimage to Solovki among the islands of the White Sea, and three times to Kiev. She used to tell of the dangers she had endured, storms and encounters with unpleasant characters; and Soloviev asked her, 'Weren't you afraid?' She replied, 'But what about God? have you forgotten him?' Soloviev, recalling this memory, concluded, 'If I feel myself constantly upheld in my most difficult moments by my hope in a higher power. I owe it to the effect produced by those words of my nurse, "What about God, then?" ' Vladimir Soloviev, the religious thinker who had so much influence on the twenteith century Russian Renaissance, the apostle of Church Unity, was the son of this historian.

This process could also happen indirectly; for popular religion by itself would not have had the power to lead back the proud intellectual in his unbelief to its own naïve faith. He had gone too far astray. But the life of the tree, when properly grafted, could still produce unhoped-for fruit. The 'graft' originated on Athos, where the practice of hesychasm had been rediscovered, and which had once again become a focus of mystical life. It was transplanted and cultivated in Moldavia by a monk from Poltava named Paissy Velichkovsky; and his disciples later introduced it into Russia. The ancient figure of the *starets* came to the fore again, and the 'prayer of Jesus' received its justification in mysticism. In fact, popular mystical devotion was revived, purified, and enriched in scores of hermitages where Paissy's followers were simple monks or superiors, going from one to another, in the Russian way, before settling. This was the ground without which renewal would have been impossible; but without this intellectual 'transplant' it could not have offered any kind of appetising fare to the cultivated world.

There was one such hermitage which possessed some particularly remarkable *startsi*: Optina Pustyn. Here began that movement which, over the years in the nineteenth century, reclaimed a section of the arrogant intelligentsia for the Orthodox Church. Kireevsky, Gogol, Dostoyevsky, Vladimir Soloviev, Konstantin Leontiev, all were, in varying degrees, disciples of the *startsi* who succeeded one another at Optina; and even Tolstoy himself, just before his death, paid one last, disburbing visit to the community.

There is a whole history to be written here, the history of the indirect but essential role that popular piety played in the Orthodox revival of the nineteenth and twentieth centuries. Suffice it here to point out the mere fact of it, so as to enable the reader better to assess the religion of the Russian people in its totality.[5]

Notes

1. Ianson, *Les starets de Valaam*, 1938, pp. 66–67; 73–75.
2. Bonch-Bruevich, *The World of the Sects*, pp. 130–131, and *The Abstinents of Moscow*, in *The Contemporary*, 1913, no. 2, pp. 299–315. See also A Pankratov, *The Seekers After God: a Survey of Religious Searchings of the Present Day*, Moscow, 2 vols, 1911.
3. Bonch-Bruevich, *The World of the Sects*, p. 206.
4. Mt. XVIIII, 9: 'If your eye causes you to sin, pluck it out'. A. Leroy-Beaulieu has a chapter on the *skopsty* in his *Empire des tsars et la Russie*, vol. III, Paris, 1889, pp. 479–495.
5. On this subjects beside the work of I. Smolitsch mentioned above, Archpriest Cheverikov's *Optina Pustyn* (in Russian, Paris, 1926, YMCA Press) should be read.

PART II

THE PILGRIMAGE OF THE MOTHER OF GOD AMONG THE TORMENTS OF HELL

INTRODUCTION

In *The Brothers Karamazov*, Dostoyevsky has Ivan mention 'a little monastic poem, translated from Greek of course' of which 'the boldness and scenic imagination are in no way inferior to those of Dante'. This is the *Pilgrimage of the Mother of God Among the Torments*. The brilliant summary which Ivan provides is the best possible inducement to read the original.

'The Mother of God visits the nether world, with the Archangel Michael as her guide among its tortures. She beholds the sinners and the punishments. There, among others, is one very curious category of sinners in a lake of fire: those who are plunged in this lake, unable ever to come out, are "from henceforth, forgotten by God"[1]—an expression of exceptional power and depth. And the Mother of God, bewildered and weeping, falls down before God's throne to beg for grace for all the inhabitants of Hell, for those she has seen, all, without distinction. Her dialogue with God is of very great interest. She kneels in supplication and will not move from her place; when God shows her the marks of the nails in his Son's hands and feet and asks her, "How shall I forgive his executioners?" she commands all the saints, martyrs, angels and archangels to fall on their knees at her side and implore God to show his grace to all the damned, without distinction. At last she obtains from God the suspension of their tortures from Good Friday to Whit Sunday each year; and the sinners at once give thanks to the Lord and cry out from the depths of Hell, "Thou art just, O Lord, thou hast judged aright!"'[2]

Ivan's intention is to justify his own poem, the famous 'Legend of the Grand Inquisitor', by means of this venerable 'little poem'. In the above summary, Ivan speaks in a slightly quizzical tone—a 'very curious category', 'of very great interest'; but it is plain that Dostoyevsky himself was aware of the true significance of the *Pilgrimage*. If it was translated from Greek into Russian and enjoyed lasting success in Russia, it is because it answered so satisfactorily to certain religious intuitions of the Russian people. The points preserved in this summary, which, after all, occurs in the course of a narrative which is fairly detailed and circumstantial, show us what these intuitions were, in the novelist's eyes. First, there is the desire that all sinners, 'without distinction', should one day be foregiven: or, if divine justice is opposed to the absolute alleviation of their suffering, that it should at least be suspended during the joyful season of Easter. And secondly, there is the immense efficaciousness of prayer in general, and more particularly of the intercession of the Mother of God.

The Pilgrimage of the Mother of God Among the Torments is an apocryphon; one, that is, of the very many narratives composed in the first Christian centuries and dealing with the 'fringes' of sacred story, since what could be read in the holy books still left some areas of curiosity unsatisfied. These stories originated and multiplied in the East, and popular imagination was given free rein in this sphere. The Jews had already elaborated the stories of characters like Abraham, Moses, Isaiah and Solomon. The Christians elaborated those of the apostles in the same way: there were 'Acts' of Peter, Thomas, and so on, and 'Gospels' of Peter, Thomas, and others, forming a huge corpus of literature which spread across the Judaeo—Christian world.

It abounds in elements of all kinds: there is much that is fanciful, some traditions which may perhaps be worthy of credence, some naïve answers to the questions of believers, reflections of various doctrines which appeared here and there. And the form as much as the content had plenty to captivate readers or listeners: stories rich in the unexpected and exotic, lively dialogue, the adventures and exploits of holy persons, and all this in a style both concrete and rich in imagery.

One subject was regularly dealt with—the last things. There were revelations, 'apocalypses', concerning the Last Judgement, the sufferings of departed souls, the condition of the blessed, the pains of the damned, the end of the world and the Second Coming of Christ. This genre of eschatological writing, originating in Judaism, is represented in the New Testament by the *Apocalypse* of St John. It flourished in the Jewish-Christian period with such works as the *Vision of Isaiah* or the *Apocalypse of St Peter*, and was further enriched in the Byzantine epoch with the *Apocalypse of St Paul* and the *Apocalypse of the Mother of*

God—which is identical with the *Pilgrimage of the Mother of God Among the Torments*.

The *Vision of Isaiah* is the last part of a composite work, the *Ascension of Isaiah*, dating from the end of the first century. The prophet is led by an angel from the earth to the seventh heaven, through the choirs of celestial powers. He asks various questions and the angel replies. This deals only with the world of the blessed—the angels, the righteous men of the Old Testament, and God himself; nothing is said about the wicked.[3]

The *Apocalypse of Peter*, dated around the middle of the second century, is more complete. Christ reveals to Peter first the torments which will afflict sinners at the end of the world, then the wonders of Heaven. The wicked will be surrounded by darkness and consumed by an inextinguishable fire. Eternal punishments will afflict various categories—adulterers, persecutors, usurers, idolaters, and so forth. They will be given up to wild animals, eaten by worms, mutilated and tormented by the demons; but they will acknowledge their punishment to be just. At this revelation, Peter weeps for a long time, and begs Christ to have mercy upon these sinners; and Christ promises to intercede for them with his Father. But he forbids Peter to tell the living of this, for fear that they will only increase their crimes.

The conclusion is obscure. It seems, however, that the pardon will be given, since Christ says, 'For the sake of those who have believed in me, I shall take pity on men'. Peter hands on this promise of Christ to his disciple Clement, together with the entire revelation he has received. He asks him only to go on 'making use of the idea of punishment by fire to frighten sinners into repentance'. Thus the text ends, the mercy of Christ having been gained, with the unknown author's charity transforming the eternity of the pains of Hell into a mere matter of pedagogic expediency.

The *Apocalpyse of Paul* may go back to the end of the fourth century. It is known to us in a great number of Slavonic manuscripts from between the fifteenth and seventeenth centuries, and also in an eighth century Latin version, obviously based upon the older Greek text that has not come down to us. These facts bear witness to the very wide diffusion of this apocryphon over the centuries in the West as well as the East. The *Apocalypse of Paul* is again a vision. An angel addresses the

59

apostle and says, 'Follow me and I shall show you the place to which the righteous are brought after their death; then I shall lead you into the pit and show you the souls of the sinners and the place to which they are brought after their death'. The apostle witnesses the judgements passed on a just soul and on a sinful soul. Then he is lifted to the third heaven, where Enoch and Elijah receive him; he travels through the various cities of paradise, in which the blessed are welcomed each according to his merits, until he comes to the heavenly Jerusalem, where King David eternally sings his Alleluia.

All the time, the dialogue between Paul and the angel continues. Both go off towards the West. 'And I saw a river of boiling fire; a great multitude of men and women were going into it, some up to their knees, some to their navels, some to their hips, others up to the hair of their heads'. Elsewhere, a bottomless gulf receives those who have despaired of the Lord. An old man has his bowels pierced with hooks by the angels of Tartarus: he is an unworthy priest. A bishop is stoned—or, following a variant, scorched with tonges of flame—because he had no mercy on the widow and the orphan. An unchaste reader has his lips and tongue lacerated. This deals with churchmen who betray their office, a class not considered in the *Apocalypse of Peter*. Usurers are eaten by worms; and there are many other punishments affecting all kinds of sinners. Each time, Paul asks, 'Who are these?' and the angel answers. Paul weeps and says, 'Why were they ever born?' The angel remarks, 'You may weep, but you have yet to see the greatest punishments'. This is a stinking cesspit in which those who 'did not confess that Christ had come in the flesh, and that the bread and cup' are his body and blood, are endlessly devoured. And in eternal ice, gnashing their teeth, are 'those who say that Christ is not risen'.

At last a cry goes up from the midst of the tormented, 'Lord God, have mercy on us!' Whereupon the heavens open and the Archangel Michael descends with the heavenly host and addresses the sinners thus: 'Day and night I cease not in my prayers for the human race ... But where are your own prayers? Where is your penitence? Weep now, then, and I shall weep with you ... it may be that the God of mercy will have pity on you and grant you some respite'. All, the sinners, Michael, and Paul, kneel in supplication to the Lord.

The Son of God descends from Heaven and says: 'My blood was

60

poured out for you . . . for your sakes I wore a crown of thorns . . . and yet you have not repented . . . However, for the sake of Michael . . . and my beloved Paul . . . for the sake of your brethren . . . and of your children who keep my commandments, and still more because of my own loving kindness, I grant you in perpetuity . . . a rest of one night and one day, on that day whereon I rose from the dead'. The sinners give thanks, but the tormenting angels remark to them, 'You have not obtained mercy . . . only the favour of a rest for one day and one night'.

In conclusion, Paul is welcomed into Heaven by the Virgin Mary, and hailed by the patriarchs, prophets, and righteous men of the Old Dispensation.

It is a captivating tale, with its accounts of the procedure for the judgement of souls, the journey through the seven heavens and the descent to Hell, but rather obscure in its detail. The great intercessor for the sufferers, the beloved of God, of angels, and of men, is the apostle Paul. 'Mary the Virgin, Mother of the Lord' appears only at the end to greet Paul, in a conclusion doubtless added after the Council of Ephesus's definition, in 431, of Mary as 'mother of God'—not 'mother of Jesus who later became God.'

The Apocalypse of the Mother of God obviously derives from the *Apocalypse of Paul*, but it is shorter, more sober, and better constructed. Its subject is not only the fate of the damned but also the intercessory power and the glory of the Mother of God, who has become the principal character. This apocryphon could have conceived only in an age in which the cult of the Virigin had reached its high watermark and its complete splendour: now it is only she who can be imagined as obtaining from the Lord any favour for those in Hell. This could not have been earlier than the reign of Justinian. On the other hand, the language suggests that we go forward to the eighth or ninth century to date the redaction. The oldest Greek manuscript to give us the text of this apocalypse is from the twelfth century, and is at Vienna (Vidobon. theolog., no. 333). Unfortunately, it is incomplete at the beginning and has several lacunae further on. We may take it to represent quite faithfully the earliest form of the story, as it is the most sober version.

Judging from the redactions discovered in manuscripts dating from the fifteenth, sixteenth, and seventeenth centuries, the apocryphon later underwent a number of different rearrangements: scenes were displaced, parts of phrase were added, and, most obviously of all, the categories of tormented sinners were multiplied. The language is revised. The descent to Hell is rounded off, in imitation of the *Apocalypse of Paul*, with a visit to Paradise by the Mother of God.[4] Finally, the Apocalypse was printed in Athens, in 1870, following one such modernised version. This was not a scholarly edition, but rather a pamphlet, easily available, and aimed at the edification of the people. It contains, after the visit to Paradise, a naïvely moralising conclusion, promising heavenly bliss 'to those who possess this holy Apocalypse and read it with awe and trembling'. This edition was reprinted in 1897. We can see from this how the *Apocalypse of the Mother of God* has remained a living influence in Greece over the centuries right up to our own day.[5]

The apocrypha, and the apocalypses in particular, spread throughout the whole Eastern Christian world, then to the West, and then among the Slavs as soon as they were introduced to Christianity. They were translated from Greek into other languages, and so well translated that several are better preserved for us in Syriac, Ethiopic, Latin or Slavonic than in their original tongue. The oldest Slavonic version of the *Apocalypse of the Mother of God*, under the more eloquent name of *Pilgrimage of the Mother of God Among the Torments*, is to be found inserted in a collection written on parchment which the palaeographers and linguists have dated to the twelfth or thirteenth century. This collection belonged to the great Russian monastery, the Troitsa-Sergei, and our apocryphon is there placed among some translations of writings by St John Chrysostom, St Basil, 'St Clement the bishop of the Slavs', and other revered writers of undeniable orthodoxy—which witnesses to the credit this work was accorded. Linguistic details show this manuscript to be of Russian provenance. A substantial number of other Russian manuscripts of the *Pilgrimage* has been noted, but all are late in date.

The considerable quantity of Slavonic versions, Bulgarian, Serbian, Russian, Ukrainian, which have come to light bit by bit, indicating origins in almost every century from the fourteenth to the nineteenth, shows the point at which it captured the imagination of the faithful, and also, no doubt, proved its use to the clergy as a tool in their ethical instruction. From the Slavonic regions it passed over even into Rumanian-speaking areas: the first translation, from the Slavonic, was made in Transylvania around the middle of the sixteenth century, and a second, from the Greek, was produced in the eighteenth. The *Pilgrimage of the Mother of God* has never ceased to hold the interest of the Orthodox races.

The Russian intellectual world discovered it only in 1857, when a critic and literary historian, A. Pypin, published an article in the important review *Annals of the Fatherland,* entitled 'Ancient Russian Literature: the Apocrypha. *The Pilgrimage of the Mother of God Among the Torments'.* The subject was treated in broad terms, as was necessary, but general considerations took up so much space that, of the twenty-five pages of the article, the last eleven only were left for the Pilgrimge itself. The whole article was original and stimulating, and must have been something of a revelation. At this point, Pypin ignored the twelfth century text, using one text dating from 1602 and others still more recent, of which he gave no exact amount. He also ignored the Greek original, but stated: 'a Byzantine origin is beyond any doubt'.[6]

In 1862, the text of 1602—taken from a manuscript in the Tolstoy Collection, now in the public library at Leningrad (XVII, no 229, Q82)—was published in Volume III of the *Remains of Ancient Russian Literature,* edited by Count Kushelev-Bezborodko. This text was accompanied with variants from the Troitsa manuscript, which made its first appearance in this way.

In fact, the twelfth-century manuscript had been discovered by I. Sreznevsky in the interval between 1857 and 1862. At the same time, the famous Slavicist Miklosich and made his contribution with the discovery of the twelfth century Greek text in the Vienna codex. This double discovery prompted the decision of the St Petersburg Academy of Sciences to publish the two texts together, and this was done at the end of 1863 in the *Proceedings (Izvestia)* of the Academy (vol. X, fasc. V, col. 551–578).

From that time on, the apocryphon entered the public sphere. During these years, Russia was living through the rediscovery of its national antituities and popular traditions by the scholars—saints' lives, the writings of the Old Believers, songs and sagas, proverbs, local dialects, the customs and traditions of the peasants, and so on. In 1863, the *Pilgrimage* appeared in yet another edition by N. Tikhonravov, in Vol. II of his *Remains of Forbidden Russian Literature.*[7] This was the twelfth-century text.

In Russia itself, no further edition of the twelfth-century text appeared; but in Rumania, B. Petriceicu-Hasdeu reproduced it, together with Sreznevski's Greek text, in his book, *Cartile poporane ale Romanilor* (vol. II, pp. 313–367). Tikhonravov's version later appeared at Lvov in 1906 in Ivan Franko's *Apocrypha and Legends from Ukrainian Manuscripts* (vol. IV, pp. 124–134). The 1602 text provided the basis for N. Gudzi in his *Selections from Ancient Russian Literature*, several times reprinted in Moscow since 1951. This is the only contribution from the Soviet period to knowledge about our apocryphon.

Neither in Russia nor elsewhere was any collation made of the manuscripts, whether Greek or Slavonic, which had come to light (and had sometimes been published, at least in part, in reviews or anthologies).[8] The Greek and Russian texts published by Sreznevski in 1863 were never checked against the manuscripts used. All the work on a scholarly edition of this apocrphon remains to be done; there has been no attempt to clarify the text of problematic passages.

The only general study bearing on the *Pilgrimage* is that of N. Bokadorov, which appeared at Kiev in 1904 in an *Anthology (Izbornik)* dedicated to T. Florinsky (pp. 39–94). This work covers too much ground—the Byzantine background, the South Slavonic background, and the Russian background, both literary and popular—to be anything but superficial. There is an interesting but far too sketchy theological and literary commentary by Ludolf Müller in the review *Die Welt der Slaven*, VI (1961), pp. 26–39. The English translation by M. R. James in his *Apocryphal New Testament* (Oxford, 1953) is made from the Greek, and the translation by R. Trautmann in his *Altrussiches Lesebuch* (1949), pp. 26–38, is incomplete.

In sum, the *Apocalypse* or *Pilgrimage of the Mother of God*, which has so delighted the faithful of so many countries and ages, and which—as I hope will be seen—is not at all deficient in purely literary beauty, has not had the treatment its deserves from the scholarly world. In what follows here, my aim has been solely to provide a translation, based on the two Slavonic texts nearest to the earliest Greek version, that is to say, the Troitsa-Sergei manuscript of the twelfth century and the 1602 manuscript. When the twelfth-century Greek text contains a phrase omitted by the Slavonic, but important in clarifying the narrative, I have included it in my translation: the Slavonic additions are distinguished by italics.

Notes

1. An imprecise quotation from §17 of the text: 'God has no more remembrance of him'.
2. *The Brothers Karamazov*, Book V, 5.
3. On this apocryphon, see Emil Turdeanu, *The Vision of Isaiah: Orthodox Tradition and Heretical Tradition*, Thessalonica, 1968.
4. The existence in the great libraries of several Greek texts, only moderately divergent, has been noted; one was found on the island of Chios.
5. There is an immense literature on the apocrypha. For a preliminary introduction, *La Bible apocryphe*, by F. A. Amiot, Paris (Fayard), 1952, may be consulted. The apocalypses of Peter and Paul are examined on pp. 287–331. E. Turdeanu has published an excellent study on 'The vision of St Paul in the literary tradition of the Orthodox Slavs', in *Die Welt der Slaven*, I (1956), Heft 4, pp. 401–430.
6. *Otechestvenniya Zapiski*, 1857, vol. CXV, Section I, pp. 335–360 (pp. 349–360 on the *Pilgrimage*).
7. *Pamyatniki otrechennoi russkoi literatury*, vol. II, pp. 23–30.
8. Ivan Franko, in his *Apocrypha and Legends*, published three 'Revelations of the Torments Which the Most Holy Mother of God Beheld', dating from the eighteenth century, whose content is far removed from the Russian *Pilgrimages*, and a fourth text, from 1897, which, on the other hand, seems to have been translated from the printed Russian text (*op. cit.*, pp. 135–172). A fifteenth century Serbian version, markedly divergent, of the twelfth century Russian text has been published by Tikhonravov in his *Remains* in 1863 (vol. II, pp. 30–39). The Transylvanian version of the Sixteenth century was published by B. Petriceicu-Hasdeu (*op. cit.*).

TRANSLATION

For the Wednesday of the fifth week in Great Lent, a legend[1] of the most holy Mother of God, *greatly edifying*, concerning the pains of Hell and their *remission*.[2] A blessing, Father!

1. The holy Mother of God desired to pray to the Lord on the Mount of Olives.[3] 'In the name of the Father and of the Son and of the Holy Ghost', said she, 'let Michael the Archangel come down'.[4]

And Michael, captain of the hosts of Heaven, came down, and four hundred angels with him, one hundred from the East, one hundred from the West, one hundred from the South and one hundred from the North. And when they had come, Michael and the angels saluted God's Favoured One,[5] saying: 'Hail, mirror of the Father! Hail, tabernacle of the Son! Hail, handmaid of the Holy Ghost! Hail, glory of the Cherubim! Hail, foundation of the Seven Heavens![6] Hail, oracle of David! Hail, you whom the angels adore! Hail, you whom the prophets foretold! Hail, highest among all who stand before God's throne!'

And God's Favoured One said to Michael the Archangel: 'Hail, captain of the hosts of Heaven! Hail, Michael, commander of all warriors, servant of the Holy Ghost! Hail, heavenly captain, glory of the sixfold host! Hail, Michael, heavenly captain, overthrower of tyrants, rightful attendant at the throne of the Lord! Hail, Michael, inextinguishable torch of light! Hail, heavenly captain, commander of all warriors, who shall sound the trumpet to wake the dead from the beginning of time! Hail, Michael, first among all the powers of Heaven, first before the throne of God!'[7]

2. When she had glorified all the angels in like manner, the Mother of God, who desired to see how the souls were tormented, said to Michael the heavenly captain, 'I beseech you, make me to know all things that are upon the earth'. The captain of the hosts of Heaven made answer,

66

'Let it be as you say, God's Favoured One; I shall reveal all things to you'.

Then said the holy Mother of God to him, 'How many kinds of torment are there in that place where Christian folk are tormented?' And Michael the heavenly captain made answer, 'These torments cannot be told'.

Then said God's Favoured One to him, 'Reveal to me all things that are in Heaven and on the earth'.

3. Then the heavenly captain ordered the angels from the North to be ready at hand; and Hell was opened. And she beheld those who were being punished in Hell, and there was there a great multitiude of men and women, and many were their laments. And God's Favoured One asked the heavenly captain, 'Who are these?'.

And the captain of the hosts of heaven said: 'These are they who did not believe in the Father[8] and in the Son and in the Holy Ghost, *but forgot God and put their faith in the creatures that God made to be our servants, and called all of them gods: the sun and the moon, the earth and the water, and the wild beasts and the serpents, the shade of a dead man or an image of stone, Trajan, Khors, Veles, Perun, these they changed into gods, and put their faith in evil demons, and to this very day they are held in this wicked darkness,*[9] and that is why they are here tormented in this way'.

4. And she saw in another place a great darkness; and Our Holy Lady said, 'What is this darkness, and who are those who dwell therein?' And the heavenly captain said, 'An abundance of souls dwell in this place'. Then said the holy Mother of God, 'Let this darkness be lifted, that I may see this torment also'. And the angels who watched over this torment replied, 'We have been charged that none of these should see the light until the appearing of your beloved Son, who is brighter than seven suns'.

And the holy Mother of God was grieved, and she lifted up her eyes toward Heaven and, *fixing her gaze upon the invisible throne of her Son,*[10] she said, 'In the name of the Father and of the Son and of the Holy Ghost, let this darkness be lifted, that I may see this torment here'.

67

And the darkness was lifted, and the seven heavens appeared: and there dwelt a multitude of people, men and women, and many were their laments, and a great noise went up. And when she saw them, the holy Mother of God said to them, shedding tears all the while, 'O unhappy folk, *accursed and unworthy*, what have you done, how have you come to be here?'

And there came no sound from them, no answer. And the angels who watched over them said, 'Why do you say nothing?' The tormented said, 'O Favoured of God, for all eternity we have never seen the light, and now we are not able to lift our eyes on high'. And when she had turned her gaze upon them, the holy Mother of God wept very greatly.

Then, seeing this, the tormented said to her, 'How is it that you have come to visit us, holy Mother of God, when your blessed Son came upon earth and never came to talk with us, as Abraham the patriarch did not, nor Moses the prophet, *nor John the Baptist*, nor the apostle Paul, the beloved of God? But you, most holy Mother of God and mediatrix, you are the defence of all Christian folk, you intercede with God himself. How is that you have visited us, *unhappy as we are?*'[11]

Then said the holy Mother of God to Michael the heavenly captain: 'What is their sin, these people?' And Michael said, 'These are they who have not put their faith in the Father and in the Son and in the Holy Ghost, nor in you, holy Mother of God; they have not desired to extol your name, or to confess that it was of you that Our Lord Jesus Christ was born, and that, when he had taken flesh, he sanctified the earth by baptism; and that is why they are tormented in this place'.

And again the holy Mother of God shed tears and said to them, 'Why did you fall victim to such illusion? Do you not know that my name is honoured by the whole creation?' And when the holy Mother of God had thus spoken, the darkness came down again upon them.

5. Then said the captain of the hosts of Heaven to her: 'Where do you wish that we go from here, God's Favoured One, to the South or to the North?' And God's Favoured One said, 'Let us go hence toward the South'. Then the Cherubim and Seraphim turned about and the four hundred angels, and led the Mother of God thence toward the South, where a river of fire was flowing out.

And there was a multitude of men and women, and they were immersed, some to their waists, some to their armpits, others to their necks and others to the crown of their heads.

And when she saw them, the holy Mother of God cried with a loud voice and asked the captain of the hosts of Heaven, 'Who are those immersed in the fire up to their waists?' And the heavenly captain replied, 'These are they who have been cursed by their father and mother, and for that they are here tormented, because they are accursed'.

Then said the Mother of God again: 'Those who are up to their armpits in the fire, who are they?' And the heavenly captain replied, 'These are they who have ill-treated and beaten their fellows, and others of them have committed fornication, and for that they are here tormented'.

Then said the most holy Mother of God: 'And those up to their necks in the fire, who are they?' And the angel replied, 'These are they who have fed on human flesh, and for that they are here tormented thus'.[12]

The holy Mother of God said: 'And those cast into the flames up to the crown of their heads, who are they?' 'And the archangel said, 'Lady, these are they who have sworn false oaths with the holy cross in their hands, saying "The holy cross be my witness!" These men, holding that cross which the angels cannot look upon without trembling, and venerate with dread, take oaths upon it, little knowing what torment awaits them; and for that they are tormented thus'.

6. And the holy Mother of God saw a man hung up by his feet, and worms were devouring him; and she asked the angel, 'Who is this? What sin has he committed?' And the heavenly captain said to her, 'This is a man who took interest on his gold *and his silver, and for that he is eternally in torment*'.

And she saw a woman hung up *by her teeth*, and all kinds of serpents came forth from her mouth and devoured her bosom.[13] And when she saw this, the Most Holy One asked the angel, 'What is this woman? *What is her sin?*) and the heavenly captain *answered and* said, 'Lady, this is one who went about among her kinsfolk and her neighbours, listening to what they said and inventing unfriendly words, so that she roused them to quarrelling; and that is why she is thus tormented'. And the holy Mother of God said, 'It would have been better for this creature if she had never been born'.[14]

7. And Michael said to her; 'And you have yet to see the great torments, holy Mother of God'. And the Holy One said to the heavenly captain, 'Let us go from hence and go to see all the torments'. And Michael said, 'Where do you wish that we go, God's Favoured One?' And the Holy One said, 'Toward the North'. Then the Cherubim and Seraphim turned about, and the four hundred angels, and led God's Favoured One thence toward the North.

And there, spread out, was a cloud of fire, and in the midst of it were beds like flame and fire, and upon them lay a multitude of men and women. And when she saw them, the Holy One sighed. And she said to the heavenly captain, 'Who are these, and wherein have they sinned?' And the heavenly captain said,'Lady, these are they who on the Lord's holy Day did not rise for the morning office, but slept on *in idleness*, like the dead, and that is why they are tormented'.

And the holy Mother of God said: 'But if someone is unable to rise, what should he do?' And Michael said, 'Listen, Most Holy One, if someone were not able to rise even if he saw his house catch fire in all four corners, *and the fire surrounding him and scorching him*, such a man would not sin'.[15]

8. And in another place she saw tables of fire, and a multitude of people, both men and women, being burned thereon. And the Most Holy One asked the captain of the hosts of Heaven, 'Who are these, and what is their sin?' And he said, 'These are they who had no respect for the priests and did not rise before them, when they came from the good Lord's church,[16] and that is why they are tormented'.

9. And the holy Mother of God beheld a tree of iron, *and on the ends of its branches were hooks of iron*, and there was a multitude of men and women hanging there by their tongues. And when she saw them, the Holy One shed tears and asked Michael, 'Who are these, and what is their sin?' And the heavenly captain replied. 'These are slanderers and sowers of discord who parted brother from brother, and husbands from their wives'. And the Most Holy One said, 'How is it possible for brother to be parted from brother?'

And Michael said, 'Listen, Most Holy One, to what I shall tell you of these people. If anyone desired to be baptised *or to do penance for his*

70

sins, they turned him away from this, instead of instructing him how to save himself. And for that they are thus tormented, for all eternity'.

10. And the Holy One saw in another place a man hung *by his four extremities*: blood was pouring out in quantities from the ends of his nails, and his tongue was bound with a flame of fire, and he could not *sigh nor* say, 'Lord have mercy upon me!' And when she saw this, the most holy Mother of God wept greatly and said, 'Lord, have mercy!' and thrice did she repeat this prayer. And there came to her the angel who had the ordering of the torments, and he set free the man's tongue. And the Most Holy One asked, 'What is this poor man who suffers such torments?'

And the angel said, 'This is a sacristan,[17] a servant of the Church, and, instead of doing the will of God, he sold the vessels which belonged to the Church, saying, "He who works for the Church must keep himself by the Church".[18] And for that he is here tormented'. And the Most Holy One said, 'As he has done, so let him suffer'. And the angel once more bound his tongue.

11. And the captain of the hosts of Heaven said, 'Come, Lady, that I may show you where the priests are tormented'. So she went, and priests hung up by the ends of their nails; fire came forth from their skulls and burned them. And when she saw this, the Most Holy One said, 'Who are these, and what is their sin?' And Michael said, 'These are they who celebrated the Liturgy and attended upon the throne of God, *pretending to be worthy*; but when they made ready the offerings, instead of treating them with care,[19] they let morsels fall to the ground, *like the good Lord's stars*.[20] At that the terrible throne was shaken and the footstool of God trembled. And for that they are tormented thus'.

12. And the Holy One saw a man, and a winged dragon which had three heads. Now two of these heads were against the man's two eyes and the other against his lips. And the Most Holy One said, 'What is this *poor* man, who cannot rest because of this dragon?' And the heavenly captain said, 'Lady, this is one who used to read the holy books to the people, while he himself did not hearken to the Gospel; he taught the people, and did not himself do the will of God, *but lived in fornication and all manner of iniquity*'.

71

13. And the captain of the hosts of the Lord said, 'Come, Most Holy One, that I may show you where the angelic and apostolic order is tormented'. And the Holy One beheld[21] a place where there were people lying on a flame of fire, and a worm which never slept was devouring them.

And the Holy One, said, 'Who are these?' And Michael replied, 'These are they who wore the mantle of angels and apostles, who were glorified upon earth by the names of patriarchs and bishops, and had the reputation of holy fathers. But in Heaven they were not called holy, for they did not act as if they wore the mantle of angels and apostles. And for that they are tormented thus.'

14. And the Most Holy One saw women hung up by all of their nails, with flames coming from their mouths and burning their whole bodies, and serpents coming out of this flame and clining to them, and they cried, 'Have mercy upon us, for we alone suffer more than all the other torments'. And the Most Holy One said, shedding tears all the while, 'What are their sins?' And the heavenly captain said, 'These are priests' wives who did not honour their husbands and married other men after their husbands had died, and for that they are tormented'.

15. And she saw other women lying in the fire, and all kinds of serpents were devouring them. And the Holy One said, 'What is their sin?' And Michael replied, 'These are nuns who sold their bodies for lechery, and for that they are here tormented'.

16. And the heavenly captain said, 'Come, Most Holy One, and I shall show you where the multitude of sinners is tormented'. And the Holy One saw a river of fire, and the appearance of this river was like a fire spreading out to devour the whole earth,[22] and in the midst of the waves was a multitude of sinners. And when she saw them, the Mother of God shed tears and said, 'What is their sin?' The heavenly captain said, 'These are the fornicators and adulterers, the thieves, those who listen in secret to what their neighbours are saying, the brawlers and slanderers, those who harvest or turn up another man's field, those who do not wait for the end of the fast,[23] those who eat the fruits of another man's labour,[24] those who come between man and wife, the drunkards,

72

the unmerciful princes, the bishops and patriarchs and tsars who did not fulfil the will of God, those who are greedy for silver, those who take interest, and those who abet evildoing'.

When she had heard this, the most holy Mother of God shed tears and said, 'Alas, poor sinners', and she said to the heavenly captain, 'What pain these sinners have! better for them if they had not been born'.

17. And Michael said to her, 'Why do you weep, Holy One? You have not seen the great torments'. And the Most Holy One said,[25] 'Guide me, that I may see all the torments' And Michael said to her, 'Where do you wish that we go from here, God's Favoured One, toward the East or toward the West, *toward Paradise on the right*, or to the left, where the great torments are?' And the Most Holy One, said 'Let us go hence toward the left'.

When the Most Holy One had spoken thus, the Cherubim and Seraphim turned about, and the four hundred angels, and they led the Most Holy One thence toward the left.

And there she saw a river of fire, and near this river was a blackdarkness: there lay a multitude of men and women, and they were boiling therein as if in a cauldron; and as it were the waves of the sea broke over the sinners and, when the waves arose, they drowned the sinners a thousand cubits deep, and they could not say, 'Have mercy upon us, you who judge justly!' Unsleeping vermin devoured them. Nothing was there but gnashing of teeth.

And when the angels who kept watch saw the Most Holy One, they all cried with one voice, 'Holy, holy, holy are you, O God; and as for you, Mother of God, we bless you, and your divine Son who was born of you; because for all eternity we have never seen the light, *but today we see the light because of you, Mother of God*'.

And again they all cried out with one voice, 'Hail, Most Favoured Mother of God! Hail, radiance of the eternal light! And hail to you also, Michael, captain of the hosts of Heaven, who intercedes with the Lord for the whole universe! For we see how the sinners are tormented and we are greatly grieved'.[26]

And the Mother of God, seeing the angels saddened and grieved because of the sinners, shed tears, the Most Holy One; and all cried out with one voice, 'In good time have you come into this darkness to see

73

what torments we are in. Pray, Most Holy One! you and the captain of the hosts of Heaven!' *And hearing the weeping and clamouring of the sinners*, they too raised their voices in weeping, crying out and saying, 'Lord, have mercy upon us!'

And when they had made their prayer, the storm in the river was calmed, and the waves of fire, and the sinners appeared, *like grains of mustardseed.*

And when she saw them, the Holy One wept and said, 'What is this river and what are its waves?' And the heavenly captain said to her, 'This river is made entirely of pitch and its waves of fire, and those who are tormented are *the Jews,*[27] those who tormented Our Lord Jesus Christ the Son of God; and all the pagans who have not been baptised[28] in the name of the Father and of the Son and of the Holy Ghost; and those who, although they were Christians, believed in demons and rejected God and holy baptism; and those who committed fornication after baptism either with their godfathers or godmothers, or with their mothers of their daughters; and poisoners who bring about men's death by giving them poison, and those who kill with weapons; *and those who smother their children;*[29] and because of this they will be tormented by reason of their deeds'.

And the Holy One said, 'As they have done, so let it be!'

And once again the storm-tossed river fell upon them with its waves *of fire, and the darkness covered them.* And Michael said to the Mother of God, 'Once a man is imprisoned in this darkness, God has no more remembrance of him'. And the Most Holy One said, 'Alas poor sinners! for the flame of this fire never eases'.

18. And the heavenly captain said to her, 'Come, Most Holy One, that I may show you the lake of fire, *that you may see where Christian folk are tormented'*. She beheld, and heard the weeping and clamouring that came from them, but it was not possible for her to see the people themselves. And she said, 'Who are these and what is their sin?' And Michael said to her, 'These are they who were baptised and received the cross in word, but did the works of the devil and let the time for repentance go by, and for that they are here tormented in this way'.

19. And the Most Holy One said to the captain of the hosts of Heaven, 'One thing only I pray you: that I too may descend to be tormented with

74

the Christian folk, *because they are called the children of my Son'*. And the heavenly captain said, 'Remain in Paradise'. And the Most Holy One said, 'I beg you, exhort the hosts of the seven heavens *and all the hosts of angels, that we may all pray for these sinners:* if only the Lord God would hear us and have mercy upon them!'

And the heavenly captain said, 'The Lord God is a living God, and great is his name! Seven times by day and seven by night,[30] when we give glory to God, *we prostrate ourselves also for the sake of the sinners, Lady, before the Lord.* But the Lord does not give ear to anything of this'.

And the most holy Mother of God said, 'I beseech you, command the hosts of angels to lift me up to the heights of Heaven and set me before the invisible Father'.

20. And the heavenly captain gave the command, and the Cherubim *and Seraphim* came forward and lifted up God's Favoured One to the heights of Heaven and set her before the invisible Father, close to his throne. And she lifted up her hands towards her blessed Son, and said, 'Mercy, Lord, for the sinners, for I have seen them and I cannot bear it: let me too be tormented with the Christians!'

And there came a voice, addressing her and saying, 'How should I have mercy on these people, when I see the marks of the nails in my Son's palms? No, I have no room for mercy toward them'.

Then said the Most Holy One, 'Lord, I do not pray you for the unbelieving Jews. But for the Christians I beseech your mercy'.

And there came a voice, addressing her and saying, 'I see that they had no mercy on their own brethren. No, I have no room for mercy toward them'.

Then said the Most Holy One, 'Mercy, Lord, for the sinners! Mercy, Lord, for the work of your hands, for in all the earth they call upon my name,[31] in all their torments and in every place across the whole earth, saying, "Lady, most holy Mother of God, help us!" And when men come into the world they say, "Holy Mother of God, help me!"'

Then said the Lord to her, 'Listen, most holy Mother of God, I shall never forsake any man who invokes your name, neither in Heaven nor on earth'.

And the most holy Mother of God said, 'Where is Moses the prophet, where are all the prophets, *and you, patriarchs, who never committed*

75

any sin? Where is Paul the beloved of God? Where is Dominica, the glory of Christians?[32] Where is the power of the holy Cross by whom Adam and Eve were saved from from the curse?'

Then Michael, the heavenly captain, and all the angels said, 'Mercy, Lord, for the sinners!' Then Moses cried, 'Mercy, Lord, for it was I who gave them your law'. Then John cried out, 'Mercy, Lord, for it was I who preached to them your gospel'. Then Paul cried out, 'Mercy, Lord, for it was I who sent your epistles to their churches'.

And the Lord God said, 'Listen, all of you! If they are judged by my Gospel or my law, or by the preaching of the Gospel which John performed and by the epistles which Paul sent, then according to this they deserve an adverse judgement'.

And the angels knew not what to say, except, 'Have mercy, for you are just, O Lord!'

And the most holy Mother of God said, 'Mercy, Lord, for the sinners, for they received your Gospel and kept your law'.

Then said the Lord to her, 'Listen, Most Holy One: if any of these had done evil and repented of his deed, then you would be right in what you say; but if they have studied my law and have done evil yet again, then, since they have not renounced evil, what should I say but what has been said—"He will repay them according to their malice"?'[33]

Then all the saints, when they heard the Lord, knew not what to answer.

And when she saw that all had availed nothing, and that the Lord had not listened to the saints but had withdrawn his grace from the sinners, the Most Holy One said: 'Where is Gabriel the heavenly captain, who once hailed me because he had been charged by the Father with this mission before all ages; now he pays no attention to sinners. Where is the giant who carries the hailstorms over his head and casts them upon the earth that is polluted by the wicked deeds of men? Then the Lord sent his Son and assured that the earth would give its fruits.[34] Where are the servants of the throne? Where is John the Divine?[35] Why have you not come forth with us to beseech the Lord for the sake of sinful Christians? Do you not see all the sinners weeping? Come, all you angels in Heaven! Come, all you righteous that the Lord has justified! It has been given to you to pray for the sinners. You too, Michael, come! You are the chief of the incorporeal spirits before the thone of God, so command all to do this: let us fall at the feet of the invisible Father, and not rise from thence until God gives ear to use and has mercy upon the sinners!'

Then Michael fell on his face to the ground before the throne, *and so did all the heavenly powers and all the orders of incorporeal spirits.*

And the Lord beheld the supplication of the saints, and he was moved with mercy for the sake of his only Son and said, 'Go down, my Son, my beloved, and behold the supplication of the saints, and show your face to the sinners'.

And the Lord came down from his invisible throne, *and beheld those who were in darkness, and they all cried out with one voice, 'Have mercy upon us, Son of God, have mercy upon us, king of all ages!'*

And the Lord said: 'Listen, all of you! I planted Paradise and created man in my own image and set him to be master in Paradise; and I gave the man and the woman life eternal. But they were disobedient and sinned by their own will, and were delivered up to death. But I did not wish to see the work of my hands tormented by the devil: I came down upon earth and took flesh of a virgin, and raised myself up on the cross to deliver them from slavery and from the primal curse; I asked for water and they gave me gall mixed with vinegar; it was my hands that created man,[36] and they put me into the grave. Then I went down to Hell and trampled my enemy underfoot, I raised up my chosen ones, I blessed the Jordan to heal you of the primal curse, yet you took no thought to repent of your sins; you called yourself Christians, but in words only, for you did not keep my commandments; and for this you are now in inextinguishable fire, and I can do no more to show you mercy. But today, by the compassion of the Father, for it is he who has sent me to you, and the prayers of my mother, for she has wept greatly for you, and the entreaty of Michael, the captain of the hosts of Heaven, and the multitude of martyrs, for they have been greatly grieved for you, this is what I shall grant you, who are tormented day and night: from Holy Thursday until Pentecost, and you will have remission; and you shall give glory to the Father and the Son and the Holy Ghost'.

And all made answer, 'Glory to your compassion!'

Glory be to the Father and to the Son and to the Holy Ghost, now and for ever, and unto the ages of ages. Amen.

Notes

1. In the etymological sense, rendering the word *slovo*, which designates any writing other than a Life or a Chronicle—a sermon, a narrative, a poem or a treatise. This 'legend' is meant for spiritual reading in monasteries—which is why Dostoyevsky calls it a 'monastic poem'—as was the Apocalypse of Paul, the latter for Thursday and the former for Wednesday in the fifth week of Great Lent.

2. The Greek has 'penitence', the Russian 'repose'. The title has at some point been altered; but it cannot refer to anything other than the 'remission' of the torments.

3. In Mt., XXIV, 3, it is on the Mount of Olives that Christ speaks of the Fall of Jerusalem and the signs of the last days. The Mount of Olives is the starting-point for the action of several New Testament apocrypha (such as *The Dream of the Mother of God*).

4. The Archangel Michael is the protector of God's people in Old and New Testaments, and of Christian souls, in the East as in the West (see the Offertory of the Requiem Mass: *signifer sanctus Michael represent at eas in lucem sanctam))*, and he plays a great part in the Apocrypha (*The Vision of Isaiah*, for instance).

5. This phrase is used throughout to translate the single Russian adjective derived from the composite word for 'divine grace'.

6. The representation of the supraterrestrial world in the form of seven heavens originated in Syria and replaced another, older model which thought in terms of three heavens.

7. The praises of the Mother of God and of Michael seem to have embarrassed the Slavonic translator, who perpetrates several confusions (unless these are to be attributed to the copyists).

8. The preceding section is given in the 1602 manuscript; the twelfth century manuscript, of which the opening is missing, begins only at this point.

9. The whole of this passage, missing from the Greek, is an ancient Slavonic interpolation; the text is already altered in the twelfth century manuscript, so the translation given is conjectural. Quite clearly, the author of the Slavonic version wished to attack the paganism of his fellow-countrymen. Khors, Veles and Perun are mentioned in the Chronicle attributed to Nestor under the years 907, 971 and

980. The Grand Duke Vladimir had, in 980, 'erected idols on the hill' at Kiev, especially one of Perun, 'made of wood, with a head a head of silver and a golden moustache'. As for Trajan, he is mentioned only in the apocryphal *Vision of the Twelve Apostles* and in the *Lay of Igor's Host*: in the southern regions, as far as the Lower Dnieper, there were many statues of the emperor who had conquered Dacia, and these were taken by the Slavonic tribes to be representations of a god.

10. Wrongly interpreting an abbreviated Greek word, the Slavonic has 'toward the angels' for 'toward Heaven'. Then, by some singular inadvertence, the writer has 'of her Father' instead of 'of her Son', in the clause which is not found in the Greek; and this error recurs in the various other manuscripts. These two slips should be noted, but there is no point in perpetuating them in translation.

11. Since, as we are about to find out, this deals with heretics who deny the dogmas of the Trinity and the Mother of God—that is, non-Christians—it is the job of Abraham, Moses, John the Forerunner, and Paul the apostle of the Gentiles to visit them. Christ was equally able to do so, in his infinite mercy. But none of them have done so; only the Mother of God has done this.

12. 'Feeding on human flesh' is explained thus in the Greek: 'And the Most Holy One said, "How is it possible for a man to eat human flesh?" And the heavenly captain said, "Listen, Most Holy One, to what I shall tell you of that. These are they who have taken their own children from the cradle and have cast them out to be the prey of dogs; or who have delivered their brethren unjustly to kings and great men. It is these who have fed upon the flesh of men, and for that they are punished".'

13. The word 'bosom' is absent from the Slavonic as it is from the Greek; it is supplied by the Athens edition of the Greek text.

14. Mt., XXVI, 24.

15. This case of conscience must have been of interest to the Slavonic Christians, for it is not absent from any version of the *Pilgrimage*. It recalls the casuistry of the 'Questions and Answers' which provide the main point of a good many apocryphal works.

16. The Greek has '. . . came *to* the church', without making clear what the subject of the verb is. The translator must have been thinking of

clergy coming from the church to the houses to give a blessing or say a prayer.

17. The Slavonic translator, failing to understand the word *oikonomos*, translates this as 'a servant of the *icons* and of the Church'.

18. I Cor., IX, 13.

19. This refers to the very first part of the Liturgy, the 'proskomidia', during which the priest sets aside from the oblations, or 'prosfora', the portion which will be consecrated and the portions which will be offered for the living and the dead. He must then gather up all the morsels on the paten so that none falls to the ground.

20. The Greek has, 'the stars fell to the earth', the 'stars' being the portions set aside from the oblations.

21. There is a leaf missing from the twelfth century manuscript at this point. The text which follows is that of the 1602 manuscript.

22. The twelfth century Greek text has '. . . like blood, and, when it has overflowed, it devours everything beneath its waves'. The Slavonic preserves 'devour' and corresponds to a more recent Greek text which reads '. . . runs over all the earth'.

23. A highly conjectural translation, following the Greek ('those who break the fast before the time'), of a phrase that has been much altered.

24. Contravening Ps CXXVIII, 2: 'Thou shalt eat the labour of thine hands: O well is thee and happy shalt thou be'.

25. Here the twelfth century text begins again.

26. From '. . . but today we see the light' onwards, only the recent Greek text corresponds to the Slavonic.

27. The Greek does not name the Jews, but has only '. . . Those who tormented . . .'

28. As in the Greek, the list as a whole requires the re-insertion of a missing negative here.

29. The sin of smothering children, voluntarily or accidentally during sleep, is provided for in the Russian manuals for confessors; the phrase is absent from the Greek.

30. The angels thus double the daily cycle of hours suggested by the Psalmist (Ps. CXIX, 164: 'Seven times a day will I praise thee').

31. The Slavonic 'your name' is, judging from what follows, a mistake. The Greek has 'my name'.

32. The equivalent of 'Dominica' (i.e. 'the Lord's Day', Sunday) is the

popular name, in Russia, as in Greece, for 'Anastasia', the personification of the Resurrection. This invocation is a popular feature of the Slavonic world; the cult of Sunday, according to Veselovsky may date from the tenth century. The Greek has 'rampart of Christians'.

33. The text of this Slavonic expansion has been somewhat altered. In particular, the translation . . . 'renounced evil' is by no means certain. One Serbian version has '. . . if they have repaid evil with evil'.

34. There is an allusion here to a legend of which the Talmud has some traces: the giant Gabriel is the angel who commands the thunder and has charge of the fruits of the earth. The whole of this passage has been greatly altered, and no Greek text is any help in emending it.

35. I.e., John the Evangelist.

36. The 1897 text adds here: '. . . and the hands of the Jews nailed me to the cross'.

COMMENTARY

Sources   No-one who has read consecutively the two 'descents into Hell' of St Paul and the Mother of God could doubt the derivation of the latter from the former. The overall pattern is the same, the categories of the damned and their punishments are similar, and many of the formulae in the dialogues and the reflections of the characters are identical. I shall not trouble to quote any more than the phrase borrowed from the Gospel, 'Better for them if they had never been born'; other instances might be cited.

However the Descent of the Mother of God is no less original a work for all this. In the most authentic texts available to us, it is not combined with an exaltation to Heaven, and there is no reason for supposing that such an episode originally stood in the text. The main character is not the apostle but the Mother of God; and this is the major novelty. In the descent of St Paul, the Mother of God only appears at the end, in a second visit to Paradise, to greet Paul, and this conclusion comes in as a late addition to the original text. In the *Pilgrimage*, the Mother of God is the central character from the very beginning. It is she, with her prayers to the Lord on behalf of the sinners, who supplies the significance of the whole work.

Ideas   If the *Pilgrimage* is intended to suggest to the faithful a solution to the difficult problem of reconciling God's justice and his mercy, when the Church (after hesitating over the interpretation of the evangelical texts) had decided on the eternity of the pains of Hell, it is clear that the Mother of God has the necessary authority for obtaining this compromise solution, a sign of indulgence from God. Thus, two themes are conflated in the narrative—the glorification of the Mother of God for her potent intercession, and a modification of the uneasily tolerated doctrine of an eternal Hell.

The Mother of God is exalted not only for her intercession, but also for her charity, which is superior to that of Abraham, Moses, John the Baptist, and Paul, and even of her own Son. She weeps at the sight of the torments; she is unmoved only by the pagans, the Jews, and some categories of Christians—the apostates, the incestuous and the murderers. She pleads the cause of the sinners with warmth, accepts no rebuff, and calls to her aid all the powers of Heaven; and God, faced with this universal supplication which she has stirred up, sends his Son to pronounce sentence: 'there is no forgiveness for those who have not kept my commandments, though they call themselves Christians; but there is mercy'.

This mercy consists of a suspension of the pains of Hell, from Maundy Thursday to Pentecost. If one looked for perfect logic in this age and this genre, it would be rather surprising that this remission includes the day of the Passion, instead of extending only over the Easter season, until Pentecost. In the *Apocalypse of Paul*, the damned are freed from their torments only on the day of the Resurrection, that is, Easter (I do not believe that this is 'every Sunday', as E. Turdeanu, *op. cit.*, p. 405, takes it to mean). This idea of the Easter remission was taken up by various writers. If the text quoted by Mark of Ephesus, the Greek spokesman at the Council of Florence in 1438, is authentic, St Basil prayed thus to God: 'Be pleased favourably to hear our supplications for those in Hell. We have sure hope that you will grant them some respite and relief'. And this prayer was intended for Easter Day. Unfortunately, this text is not found among the extant works of St Basil.

The desire for some mitigation of the pains of Hell has quite often been expressed, in a more general way. St Augustine does not categorically reject the idea that 'God, while he sets no period to eternal punishment, accords it some relief or intermission' (*Enchiridion*, P.L.XI, 284, 5).

In any case, the great sinners go on being punished, in our apocryphon, and this answers to another concern of the faithful. God no doubt permits evil; but he takes vengeance for it also. The imaginative recounting of such vengeance is a source of solace and joy to the people. It is unquestionably the problem of evil which, in the thought of Dostoyevsky's Ivan Karamazov, establishes a relation between our apocryphon and the Legend of the Grand Inquisitor.

Composition   The composition is not rigorous, but a prologue and a conclusion are clearly in evidence. The prologue is the dialogue between the Mother of God and the Archangel Michael who is summoned by her (1 and 2). The conclusion begins with the Mother of God's return to Heaven and her supplication, and ends with the Lord's decision and the *Gloria* of acknowledgement from all those around (19–20).

In the account of Hell, it is possible to distinguish a first area, to the West, where pagans and heretics who did not believe in the Trinity, and refused to honour the Mother of God, are located. Because they have not accepted the light, their punishment is to remain in darkness (3–4).

Next comes a region to the South, where we find Christians who have lost the chance of salvation for 'formal' reasons: those who have been cursed by their fathers and mothers, those who have offended against natural or spiritual kinship, perjurers, usurers, and slanderers. They receive a variety of punishments (5–6).

In the North are the 'great torments', reserved for those who have sinned against the Church: those who are lazy about coming to services, those who do not respect priests, those who draw their brethren away from the sacraments (7–9). Next come the wicked servants of the Church: the sacristan who steals the sacred vessels, the reader whose conduct contradicts the texts he reads, the priest who celebrates negligently, the unworthy bishop, the priest's wife who remarries, nuns who are unfaithful to their vows (10–15).

After these special categories, it is the turn of 'the multitude of sinners', fornicators, thieves, drunkards, troublemakers, usurers, and so forth, not an exhaustive list, no doubt, but one in which lay and clerical potentates are not forgotten (16).

Here there occurs a change of direction 'toward the North': a river of fire in which Jews, apostates, committers of incest, and poisoners are boiling; a lake of fire for the baptised who have given their souls to the devil and remained unrepentant. The impression is given that these are the greatest criminals: they are forgotten by God (17–18).

This is, roughly, the organisation of the *Pilgrimage*. We cannot, then, speak of it as totally without order, though from our point of view as Latins and modern men, there is no lack of incoherences, or obscurities in detail. The author or authors were not concerned with the exact

84

classification of sins nor with the adaptation and gradation of the torments. We can only conclude that they had in view those crimes or faults which were common in the life of their times—the mother who suffocates her child in her sleep for lack of precautions, gossip among neighbours, incestuous relationships within a large and undivided family, the moving of boundary markers to encroach on as adjoining field . . . Of course, an element of social protest also makes itself felt: among the damned are bishops and patriarchs, princes and tsars—in short, all those perennially hateful figures who betray the charge entrusted them.

It is noteworthy that the sins which are punished concern not genuine morality but external conduct. There is nothing about the egotistical, the proud, the envious, and so on, but only those guilty in terms of civil or ecclesiastical law. This suggests that the *Pilgrimage* has passed through the formalist hands of a churchman who was a professional canonist and something of a casuist.

Literary Value The *Pilgrimage* in the twelfth-century text, Greek or Slavonic, has a notable sobriety, and from this derives the dramatic power which one cannot fail to recognise in it. One cannot long remain insensitive to the grandeur of the debate between the Mother of God, supported as she is by all the spirits, and her Son, who has a personal interest at stake. The sorrows he lays at the door of mankind recall the *Improperia* of the Latin Liturgy of Good Friday. It is a tragic lawsuit between sinful men and the Crucified, who is both judge and plaintiff. For it is not only the damned who are concerned here: we must see behind them—as Ivan Karamazov, and, even more, his creator, must have done—the whole of humanity immersed in suffering, whether by its own fault or not.

The impressive character of the authentic text is thrown into sharp relief by comparison with the developments added to it over the centuries.

Various Amplifications and Accretions In the seventeenth-century texts examined by Pypin, there is already a prominent place among the damned allotted to 'unmerciful judges', 'wicked Judges who condemn the righteous and acquit the guilty', to 'princes and lords who keep men in slavery and torture them again all justice'. There is more realism here, in this moving protest by the downtrodden common people, but less majesty. But it is most particularly in the eighteenth century Ukrainian versions collected by Franko that amplifications of all kinds abound without measure.

The damned cry, 'Oh, oh, oh! woe!' The punishments are made more exact, the scenes more complicated: some of the damned hang with their heads downwards; others have wild beasts loosed upon them, each with three heads, to tear out their hearts or sever their veins; there are cauldrons with brimstone and pitch boiling in them. The tally of sinners is extended, as if for fear of forgetting any: Jews and Greeks, Nero, Nestorius, Diocletian, Herod, Decius, the soldiers who scourged Christ, wizards, soothsayers, sorcerers, hoarders of gold and silver, millers who give false weight, land-surveyors who give false measure, labourers who steal seed, smiths who make off with iron, weavers who cheat over thread or cloth, robbers of beehives. The 1897 text, which follows the original fairly closely, nevertheless retains a mention of those who surreptitiously bribe judges, misers who do not pay their labourers the agreed wage, and husbands who break their oaths by abandoning their wives.

The revised and augmented *Pilgrimage* also contains some *genre* scenes. It falls to St Michael to venture a dubious joke. When the Mother of God, seeing the punishment endured by those who have not fulfilled their religious duties, asks in astonishment, 'What? so many people in good health not wanting to go to church?' the archangel replies, 'Ah well, they have a devil in their heads, another sitting on top of them, and a third holding their legs'. The seriousness of the ancient text is thus jeopardised by the abuses of storytellers who are either over-imaginative, or over-eager to censure their contemporaries.

In Russia the *Pilgrimage* also served, until the end of the nineteenth century, as a vehicle of popular protest against the innovations, scandalous and oppressive at the same time introduced by Peter the Great, and further aggravated by his successors. If we are to believe Archpriest Malov, writing in 1833 against the Old Believers, these groups had put their own version of the *Pilgrimage* into circulation, in which the damned were parents who taught their children the Latin alphabet, townspeople who yoked their horses with a pole in the Western manner, those who cut their beards and moustaches and intoxicated themselves with smoking, and foreign stewards who overloaded the serfs with work, who mercilessly extorted rents from them and sent their sons to the army. Wicked landlords are eaten by dragons, and so are cruel who tormented their maids. The text in question ends with this bit of advice: anyone who carries the *Pilgrimage* with him will have his sins forgiven, but whoever pays no attention to it and does not pay the scribe who copied it will be delivered up to eternal torments, gnashing of teeth, ice and fire. If Malov's account is true, we see here to what point our venerable apocryphon degenerated in certain cases.

The torments of the damned provided inspiration for the writers of the 'Spiritual Songs' recited by wanderers, beggars and blind men as part of their musical repertoire among the crowds on the great pilgrimages. In an article in *Russian Thought* (December, 1915), one such blind man relates how their party, guided by a child, arrived some time before the war at a town on the day of its patronal festival and sang the 'Friday Legend' or 'how the Mother of God visited the torments'.

These torments, together with various legendary tales, also furnished a subject for crudely illustrated coloured broadsheets (which in Russia were the equivalent of popular thrillers). They also form part of the depictions of the Last Judgement which, since the twelfth century, have been painted on the lower West wall of churches for the instruction of the faithful, following the recommended pattern for artists: 'All sinners in holy orders or monastic vows have their lower parts in a cauldron; liars are hung by their tongues, actors by their navels. The punishment for princes, boyars, and judges is a worm which never sleeps; that for usurers and money-grubbers, devils pouring molten gold and silver down their throats ... Those who have committed fornication with priests' wives or nuns or caretakers of churches, or with godparents or sisters are hung up over the fire by their backbones'.

These last details are, quite clearly, echoes of our *Pilgrimage*. The deep impression produced in the popular imagination by these pictures of the Last Judgement is reflected in Ostrovsky's play, *The Storm* (1859).

PART III

THE RESISTANCE OF THE RUSSIAN PEOPLE TO PERSECUTION

1. PERSECUTION

The Russian Church has been persecuted since 1917. During the half-century which has elapsed, this persecution has not ceased for an instant; all it has done is to take on diverse forms, evolving from its earlier and bloodier manifestations into 'dissuasion', from juridical sanctions into 'education', from open war into contemptuous compromise. Various methods have been employed at the same time—some more than others, according to the times; and it is this which gives the impression of an alternation between periods of relaxation and periods of intensification. There are no periods of peace.

This persecution requires careful definition, since it has no parallel in history. It is not simply an anticlerical campaign like that of the Combes era in France or the *Kulturkampf* in Germany; nor is it a policy, such as has often appeared over the centuries, directed at reducing the powers and privileges of the Church for the profit of the State; nor is it a violent but short-lived crisis, such as occurred under the Roman Emperors or occasionally in the mission field. This is a quite different matter. The Soviet State is engaged in putting into practice a doctrine of its own, Marxism, which rejects religion absolutely. So this State, insofar as it is Marxist, has as its aim the destruction of religion as such, even when it proclaims itself neutral, as in the 1918 constitution ('freedom of religious and antireligious propaganda is recognised for all citizens'). It sets out to extirpate all traces of the religious mentality in its people; and this object has not changed from the creation of the Soviet State up to the present day. It can be neither altered nor abandoned; it is the avowed and explicit aim of the Communist Party. The distinction maintained between the Party and the State means only that the latter can select the ways and means best suited for this object, according to circumstances.

At first, in 1918, this effort was restricted to the expulsion of the Church from the State, under the guise of 'separation', its expulsion from public life, education and the press, and the expropriation of all its private property; churches and objects necessary for worship were left, precariously, in the possession of the faithful. Private chapels were closed. Religious instruction was forbidden in all schools and tolerated only in private.

All contraventions of this edict were, of course, designated as counter-revolutionary. While local authorities initiated all kinds of excesses—the closure or demolition of churches, the confiscation of valuable objects, interference with worship, and arbitrary arrests of clergy. In December of 1918, these excesses were condemned by the Commissar for Justice; but the same Commissar, in March 1919 and August 1920, himself attacked the cult of relics in printed circulars, and ordered at first the opening of all reliquaries, and later their transference to museums. These operations were meant to show both the absurdity of belief in the incorruptibility of the bodies of holy men, and, consequently, the mendacity of the priests. This was a serious interference with worship and an insult to the people's religion.

The civil war provided an occasion for stepping-up the arrest and execution of 'counter-revolutionaries'. All the clergy were classed with 'non-workers', and, as a result, deprived of civil rights; so, during the period of rationing, it was virtually impossible for them to feed, clothe and house themselves, and educate their children, virtually impossible indeed, for them to live at all. They were relegated to the pariah class (*lichentsy*). However, war had not yet been declared against religion as such. The new régime had too much to do, what with the civil war, the Polish war, the revival of the economy and the establishment of the administration, to concern itself actively with ideological questions. Their turn came at the end of 1922. In November of that year, scores of the most notable-anti-Marxist thinkers or writers were exiled from Russia. And then famine furnished the pretext for a violent campaign against the Church, which was to develop into full-scale war. Invoking the need to buy grain from abroad to help the hungry, the Soviet regime ordered, on the 26th of February 1923, the confiscation of all valuable objects which had thus far been left in the churches. The Patriarch, who, since the 19th, had been urging parishes to send financial relief to the needy, so long as consecrated objects were not touched, now confirmed his prohibition against handing over such things. The faithful themselves opposed this measure; to avoid sacrilege, they were prepared to offer the cash value of the sacred objects. The devout proceeded to demonstrate their loyalty, and there were many revolts, one particularly serious one on the 15th of March in the little village of Shuya in the Kostroma province.

A memorandum of Lenin's to the members of the Politburo, dated the 19th of March, reveals to us the real intentions of the authorities in this affair. In effect it says: as soon as acts of cannibalism occur among us, this will be an excellent moment for making the great majority of the populace, and our enemies abroad as well, accept 'our expropriation of the hundreds, perhaps thousands of millions of gold roubles' still withheld by the Church, 'without which the functioning of the State in general and economic reconstruction in particular are unthinkable'. So it is necessary 'to crush all kinds of resistance with merciless energy'; at Shuya in particular, as many as possible should be arrested, 'several score at least', members of the clergy, artisans or merchants and burgesses, and 'oral instructions given to the legal authorities to conduct their trials with the maximum despatch and regard themselves as under obligation to conclude them with the execution of a large number of the most influential and dangerous reactionaries', not only in Shuya, but, if possible, in Moscow also and other ecclesiastical centres.[1]

At Shuya, eight priests and three laymen were condemned to death, and twenty-six received prison sentences. There were twelve death sentences in Moscow, and in Petrograd the Metropolitan Venyamin was shot on the 12th of August, together with an archimandrite and two laymen. Lenin's instructions had been obeyed.

At the same time, the Church was attacked internally. The Soviet State supported a group of priests styling themselves the 'Living Church' against the Patriarch Tykhon; this group called a council, declared the abolition of the Patriarchate, and began to take control of dioceses and parishes, while the authorities arrested those clergy who remained loyal. By the end of 1923, sixty-six bishops had been imprisoned or deported by these means. Here again, however, the attempt soon ran up against the resistance of the faithful. When the Patriarch Tykhon died on the 7th of April, 1925, his funeral was attended by sixty-nine bishops and an immense crowd. On the other hand, the innovators were split into three groups; they failed signally to reunite themselves, and although they were supported by the authorities, and kept up the appearance of being the official Church until 1927, the people abandoned them. The government, which had successively arrested two *locun tenents* of the Patriarchate, Pyotr and Sergei, freed the latter and allowed him to convene a provisional synod. The 'Renewed Church' declined; but, on the other hand, Metropolitan Sergei had been obliged to sign a declaration of Soviet loyalism, so extreme as to be practically scandalous, which led a number of bishops to refuse him obedience. Hence there came to be three jurisdictions: the modernist schism, a legalised but compromised Orthodoxy, and the traditionalist party, driven into a clandestine existence. The regime had succeeded in dismembering the body of the Church and destroying the hierarchy.

However, the authorities understood that they were faced not with a hundred or so prelates and a few tens of thousands of priests who could be martyred or corrupted, but with tens of millions of believers, with whom no amount of violence would succeed. The schism had failed: the people remained faithful to the Great Church. And so a massive campaign was planned: the Church was to be recognised, so as to avoid the spread of a secret religious movement, which would be more dangerous, but it was to be enclosed in a legal straitjacket which deprived it of all means of defence, and, at the same time, unrelentingly harassed by various assaults, in such a way as to weaken, stifle, and finally annihilate it. The aim was announced: by the end of the first five-year plan (1932), there must not be a single church left in Russia.

The armoury of devices tried since 1918 continued to be used. Apostasies from the priesthood were encouraged and financially rewarded; and, at the other extreme, priests marked out by their influence and enthusiasm were arrested and deported. Churches, especially the larger ones, were temptied of objects of worship without notice, on diverse pretexts, and then (behind the shelter of a barricade) converted into cinemas, libraries, or warehouses, or rapidly demolished. Feasts like Christmas and Easter were disturbed with riotous demonstrations, masquerades with mocking placards, or invasions by young Communists. Then it would be decided somewhere that bell-metal was necessary for industrialisation, and bells were everywhere taken down. One day, some atheist might think it would be a splendid act of irreligious faith if the people of a village or a factory all together brought their domestic icons to be burned in public; and everywhere

94

similar *autos-da-fé* would be organised. No legal obligation attached to this sacrifice of icons, but a kind of moral constraint was created by many means—newspaper articles, speeches from people in positions of authority, highly commended examples—and it required much courage to resist this. What dramatic scenes there must have been within families, between husbands and wives, parents and children!

It would be hard to give any precise date to these various manoeuvres in the war against religion, as they went on for the most part simultaneously. However, we do know what the major weekly paper, *Bezbozhnik* (*The Unbeliever*), and the *Ateist* publishing house were founded in 1922; in 1924, an antireligious 'University of the Air' was initiated, and the 'League of Militant Godless' began in 1925; in 1927, a *soi-disant* scientific review, *Antireligioznik*, appeared. In 1928, the schools, which until then had been officially neutral, were compelled to teach atheism: this must have occasioned great anguish for many men and women devoted both to their task of teaching and to their faith. Atheism in all its forms was inculcated in the populace: antireligious museums with guided tours, conferences, courses of various lengths for the training of specialist propagandists. In 1930, 16,000,000 editions of antireligious pamphlets or books were issued. By 1931, 5,000,000 had enrolled in the ranks of the 'Godless'. All the sciences were pressed into service for these activities—astronomy, paleontology, biology, chemistry, medicine, ethnography, history, and so on, all leading to the same conclusions: the clergy were vicious exploiters, without real convictions; beliefs were absurd and unfounded, sacraments unhygienic, rituals magical survivals, the holy books legendary, Christ a mythical personage who had never existed, and the whole history of Christianity through the ages a succession of crimes and monstrosities. The gospel ethic itself was mocked and condemned as contrary to the class struggle. Everything was manipulated towards implanting in people's minds the idea that only the mentally retarded could still be believers. Religion was constantly listed with alcholism or insanity as a fault or a disgraceful infirmity.

Such was the attack. As for the position imposed by the law on the hunted enemy of the State, it is summed up in a statute, of perfect formal regularity, promulgated on the 8th of April, 1929, and supplemented by 'instructions' on the 16th of January, 1931, and a cir-

95

cular from the Commissariat of Finance of the 20th of February, 1931. Citizens of any one persuasion and over eighteen years of age were allowed to form a religious society, on condition of applying for registration with a list of at least twenty constitutive members. If registration was granted, the society was to elect three officials by a show of hands and submit a list of all its members and ministers. After this, it could obtain by contract the free use of a building and objects for public worship. It had no right to plead in court, engage in any commercial activity (even the making of votive candles or the printing of religious or moral publications), organise funds for mutal aid, meetings or study-group (even for bible-studies, manual work, or religious teaching), open a library or provide medical services. Religious societies could charge subscriptions and receive free-will gifts, but only from their own members and exclusively for the maintenance of places of worship and ministers. The latter's sphere of activity was limited to the locality in which the place of worship was situated. A large number of clauses provide for the liquidation of the religious society or the place of worship, in case, for example, of need for repairs, bad maintenance by the society, non-payment of insurance, or the decision of higher authority. Nowhere in this document is any mention made of the Church and its hierarchy. There is reference only to parishes: religious societies already in existence must apply for registration within one year. One clause recalls that no religious teaching is tolerated in any educational establishment. Special courses in theology may be organised, but only by 'citizens of the USSR, on special permission being given'.

The meaning of this basic piece of legislation was spelled out in the amendment of the 22nd of May, 1929, to the Constitution: article 13's 'freedom of religious and antireligious propaganda' was replaced by 'freedom of religious profession and antireligious propaganda'. A little later, an official commentary added: 'From now on, all propaganda or agitation conducted by representatives of religion or the Church . . . falls outside the limits of the freedom of profession allowed by the law and comes within the scope of articles 58.10 and 59.7 of the Penal Code . . . The activity of religious societies must confine itself to public worship'. In this way, the Church was deprived of all means of defence, although everything possible was mobilised against her. Such is the regimen to which it is still subjected today.

The year 1929, with the five-year plan and the campaigns for industrialisation and collectivisation, saw the beginnings of a recrudescence of persecution. A new weapon against believers was invented: the continuous working week, decreed on the 27th of August. There was to be no more general rest on Sundays. For greater security, the newspapers no longer indicated even the days of the week. Any absence from work on a Sunday, except by twisting the rules, marked you out as a believer. On Easter Eve, every establishment organised parties, film-shows, dancing and singing to make quite sure that no workers, schoolchildren, or official and administrative personnel went to Matins and Mass; and although attendance was not compulsory, it was warmly encouraged by the authorities—the local group of 'Godless', the committee of the Soviet, the Communist Party cell, or Komsomol. Not infrequently, priests were harrassed: not only were they deprived of food ration cards and medical aid, but they were hounded out of communal dwellings. Their income was taxed arbitrarily, and their children were excluded from secondary and higher education.

An added incentive was given to the destruction of churches: in rural areas, the same vote that decided on the collectivisation issue required in general terms (according to instructions received) an abandonment of the Church, no account being taken of the opinions of believers. Religious buildings were systematically charged with indemnities; in the towns a land tax assessed at the rate of value of the real estate involved; in the country, a quota for the purchase of tractors, and the delivery of agricultural produce, although the church itself held no land; in both places, extraction of copyright charges on music performed, although there would be no author to pay. If these sums were not paid, and if the work of maintenance or repair was not carried out, the contract of usage was withdrawn and the church closed; which was the desired end.

It should further be noted that from 1918 to 1943 not one religious book was printed—no catechisms, no Bibles, saints' lives, or New Testaments: and those which existed in public places were confiscated and destroyed, or, in the great libraries, made inaccessible. At the present time, it is still prohibited to bring a copy of the Gospel into the USSR.

The conduct of the persecution was accompanied by so many

excesses, even in relation to the decree of the 8th of April, that on the 14th of March, 1930, the Central Committee of the Party censured 'inadmissible deviations' introduced 'into the struggle against religious prejudices', and, in particular, 'the administrative closure of churches without the consent of the majority of the population'. Closures and other acts of violence continued unabated until the end of 1932; but, as religion still existed, it became necessary to defer its total 'liquidation' to the end of the second five-year plan, in 1937. The constitution of 1936, which restored political rights to 'non-workers', and so to the clergy, reaffirmed the prohibition of religious 'propaganda'. But when it appeared that liquidation still lay in the future, persecution was once more unleashed in all its forms, even the bloodier ones, in 1937; and it was to last until June of 1941, the date of Hitler's attack on Russia.

Since then, the persecution has passed through still further phases of relaxation of intensification which it is not my intention to relate. I have thought it sufficient to review the weapons employed against Chistianity, before examining how the Christian populace attempted to ward off these blows.[2] The events dealt with in both these fields were, almost without exception, efforts made during the period we have been considering.

Notes

1. Although this memorandum is not included in the *Complete Works of Lenin,* reference is made to it in vol. 45 of the 1964 edition, pp. 666–667.
2. I have made extensive use of the very reliable and balanced work of Nikita Struve, *Les chrétiens en URSS,* Paris, 1963. John Skelton Curtiss, *The Church in the Soviet Union (1917–1956),* Boston, 1950, may also be consulted; it s a very well-informed work, but shows extreme indulgence toward the Soviet authorities. Similarly, Paul B. Anderson, *People, Church and State in Modern Russia* (London, 1944), constantly makes excuses for the persecutors. *Le mouvement antreligieux en URSS (1917–1932),* by René Martel, Paris, 1933, deliberately takes the side of the Soviet Government. *La guerre antireligieuse* and *Le front antireligieux en Russie soviétique,* by Mgr d'Herbigny (two pamphlets, Paris, 1930), deal with the 'campaign' of

Christmas 1929 and April to November, 1930. *Le sentiment religieux en URSS* in *Russie et Chrétienté*, September, 1935 (Centre dominicain *Istina*), pp. 105–153, includes a number of texts from Soviet publications.

2. THE ATTITUDE OF THE HIERARCHY

What has the Church's attitude been, faced with this persecution? First, there is the attitude of the hierarchy. The Patriarch Tykhon, in 1918, issued condemnations, and calls to defence, and outlined a programme of resistance. Again, in 1922, he protested against the seizure of sacred vessels. And then, on the 28th of June, 1923, a formal retractation, a kind of political acknowledgement of the regime, was published over his name in *Izvestia*. But since this document had been drawn up while the Patriarch was under arrest, public opinion saw in it no more than a forced recantation and remembered only the anathemas that had gone before.

The same intransigent attitude was shown by the Metropolitan Pyotr, whom the Patriarch had designated his successor, and, after Pytor's arrest on the 23rd of December, 1925, it was continued by one party among the hierarchy, who considered that compromise with the atheist regime would be a betrayal of the Church and of the innumerable bishops, priests and laymen martyred for the faith. Moreover, faced with a State resolved on the destruction of religion, such a compromise would be ineffectural. In short, the only thing to do when confronted with persecution was to envisage an underground life for the Church and commit it to Providence.

In contrast, other bishops hoped that a policy of submission, securing even a precarious legality for the Church, would make possible the continued existence of worship and clergy, facilitate the loyalty of the mass of Christians, and allow the Church to await better days. Metropolitan Sergei, *locum tenens* of the patriarchal throne, committed himself to this path and followed it to the furthest limits, publicly denying the reality of the persecutions and even the arbitrary closures of churches: though in this he was almost immediately given the lie by Stalin and Rykov in person.[1]

These two tendencies were present at all levels of the hierarchy.

There were priests and parishes loyal to Pyotr who refused to pray for Sergei; others, while accepting mention of Sergei in their prayers, regarded themselves as being in communion with Pyotr and his successors; a third group was obedient to Sergei. Of course, in the great wave of extermination in 1929–1933, it was Pyotr's churches that were the first to disappear. The surviving places of worship found themselves, accidentally, as it were, in Sergei's party.

In one sense, this conception of 'policy' has triumphed; we have been witnessing its application since 1943. Sergei himself became Patriarch, and the Orthodox Church now plays its part in alliance with the Soviet Government. The intransigents certainly have not disappeared, but they have been reduced to an illegal and furtive existence. But the question is: which conception has done more to preserve Christianity up to now? The supporters of Sergei's policy claim that, without his diplomacy, not the smallest kernel of Christianity, and, therefore, not the least basis for reconstruction, would have remained. It was the skill of the new Patriarch and later of his successor Alexei which compelled the Soviet State first to allow some shrines and priests to carry on, and then allow the Church that 'freedom' which it now boasts of enjoying.

It is far from easy to reply to this question, which divides the Orthodox of the emigration as much as those in Russia. In any case, this is a suitable point at which to ask, before going any further, what was the conduct, not of the hierarchy, but of the people, when confronted with persecution?

Note

1. Even the Bulletin of the Permanent Central Commission for Cults (no. 2, 1932) acknowledged the excesses committed, while attributing them to the local authorities.

3. PASSIVITY?

It seems at first sight that the Russian people displayed an astonishing, indeed scandalous, passivity in the face of persecution, offering no revolt or resistance. That would be too unqualified an impression. There have been local revolts, never mentioned in the Press. In 1922, at the time of the seizure of sacred objects in the Churches, 1,414 cases of rebellion were duly registered. Some parishes resisted the closure or demolition of their church: we shall never know how many. All such resistance, the more heroic for being useless, was quelled with bloodshed.[1]

But this impression of passivity is not entirely false. It conforms to the Russian psychology, this yielding before the application of force, this external and bodily submission—yet not without the survival of opinions, feelings, and internal steadiness. I have watched the people of Moscow, to all appearances quite unmoved, witnessing the destruction of their most venerated shrines—the Iberian Virgin, Our Lady of Kazan, or the Church of the Saviour—and renouncing their most holy objects with every semblance of indifference. They will take off their baptismal crosses and bring their domestic icons to the bonfire. They tolerate in the middle of Moscow the famous inscription, 'Religion is the opium of the people'. They will vote with a show of hands for the suppression of Sunday, for work on the holy days of Easter or Christmas, or for the conversion of their parish church into a cinema or dining-hall . . .

And yet the truth must be stated that the persecutions described have never been the work of the people. It has never been heard said that the clergy have been molested or even mocked in the street: the proof of this is that they have always been able to walk around in ecclesiastical dress. The riotous parades put on at the time of church services were the work of pseudo-military groups trained by the Young Communists.[2] The closures of churches were never desired by the people, even when they were the result of the 'unanimous' vote of a communal assembly terrorised by an agitator from headquarters. From time to time, the authorities recognised the violence done to the people in this way; Stalin did so in his address of the 2nd of May, 1930, *The Intoxication of Success.*

No more did the people follow the initiators of schism: the 'Living Church' had hardly more than a skeleton structure, and very few genuine believers: ambitious clergy or churchwardens rather than the pious womenfolk or the peasantry, as Anderson observes (p. 65). Insofar as they retained their faith at all, the people remained loyal to the authentic Church of Patriarch Tykhon. We might more accurately say that, if it applied only to the people, the situation described by an *Izvestia* correspondent on the 2nd of February, 1922, might be translated into permanent and general terms:

'It is a great rarity in our rural areas to find a Communist who does not have an icon on the wall at home. Religion and Communism get along together very well. Here are some facts. A Communist in the village gets married. The whole wedding procession goes off to the church. Leading the way is the red flag with the inscription "Workers of all lands, unite!" Then come the icons, then the groom, with a red sash, etc., across his chest. These "red weddings" are far from rare in the countryside. The *muzhik* understands Communism and the Soviet régime in his own way, and "loves" it, as he prays to God for it. In the town of Tikhanka in the Voronezh province, the whole borough asked the parish priest to celebrate a requiem on the anniversary of the October Revolution for the dead soldiers of the Red Army. The priest not only agreed, but concluded the ceremony with a brief service in honour of the Communist Party committee in the district. At Stary-dubovoi in the Zadonsk region, the priest wears a red star and has played L. Andreev's "Savva" on stage. The local peasants call him "the red parson".'

So, even among the Communists (wherever dogmatism has not killed feeling in them) and, with stronger cause, among the people at large, there is no hostility towards the Church, certainly nothing comparable to what happened during the French Revolution or in the days of 1830. Here already, then, is a definite conclusion, though a negative one. It remains to ask whether we can establish any more positive signs of the persistance of faith. Passivity is not always incompatible with an unusually durable confession of belief: although the example which follows deals with nuns, such women are very close to the people, and the story is very much in the popular tradition.

Notes

1. Anderson, pp. 52–53, quotes the case of the little town of Kimri.
2. This fact is recognised by R. Martel, pp. 72–73.

4. THE MARTYRS

This story comes from an old convict in the Solovki Islands. 'In 1929', he recalled, 'we saw about thirty nuns coming ashore. We gathered from various hints that they came mostly from Shamordino, the neighbouring convent to Optina Pustyn, made famous by Tolstoy's visits to his sister there. Their arrival in the camp provoked an exceptional incident: during the registration formalities they refused to reply to the usual questions—surname, forename, patronymic, date and place of birth, education, profession, legal record. They would only call themselves by their names in religion—Mother Maria, Mother Anastasia, Mother Yevgeniya. Great crisis, threats and all: but it was impossible to get anything else out of them. They were sent to the cells, subjected to all the worst tortures, hunger, thirst, lack of sleep, and beaten without mercy. But they stood firm.

'Then, worse still, they refused to work. A little later, I was sent for, with another prisoner who was a doctor, by the head of the health service. He asked us to examine these nuns, and gave us to understand that the wish of all concerned was to see them pronounced unfit for work: then they could be officially exempted and discipline would be preserved. "They're fanatics", said the head of the health service. "Looking for martyrdom, I should say . . . masochistic psychopaths . . . But they do make you feel sorry. I can't stand seeing their meekness and submissiveness when people hit them—and I'm not the only one. Vladimir Yegorovich (the camp commandant), he's the same. He wants to arrange things properly. So if you diagnose them as unfit, they'll be left in peace".

'My colleague declined the request, so I went on my own to examine these nuns. The women I saw were very dignified, calm and poised, in black habits much used and darned but quite clean. There were about thirty of them, all much like one another; you'd have said they were all under thirty years old, though there were certainly some younger and

105

some older. They all looked as if they'd been specially selected physically fit, with solid and harmonious figures, healthy and clean, like those white mushrooms that no worm can bite through. Fine Russian women, in short, the kind the poet talks about:

> "She will stop a cantering horse,
> And walk into a house on fire"

'Their faces all wore an expression of restrained and guarded sorrow. In their presence, you could not but feel admiration and tenderness.

'The official who should have been witnessing the visit said to me, "I'll be off so as not to bother you". This man, with his secret-police soul, was so far sensitive to the spirit of purity and modesty emanating from these nuns. I was left alone with them.

' "Good day, sisters", I said, bowing respectfully.

'They replied with a deep bow from the waist.

' "I'm a doctor, and I've been sent to examine you".

' "There's nothing wrong with us. It isn't worth the trouble of examining us", several voices interjected.

' "I am a believer, and I was arrested for my faith".

'Again several voices said, "God be praised!"

' "I understand your trouble, and I have no intention of examining you. Just tell me what you are suffering, so that I can decide how fit you are for work".

' "We're not suffering anything, we're perfectly well".

' "But you could be given specially difficult jobs . . ."

' "We won't do any jobs, difficult or easy".

' "Why?"

' "Because we don't want to work for Antichrist".

' "What's that? There are plenty of bishops and priests here, deported because of their faith, and they're all working as hard as they can. For instance, take Bishop Victor of Vyatka—he's an accountant in the naval store-room. And there are plenty of priests in the fisheries department, weaving nets—that was the apostles' job, after all. Every Friday they spend the night at work, to get ahead with the next day's work, so that they have Saturday evening and Sunday morning free".

' "We don't know them", replied one of the eldest nuns, very gravely;

"We condemn no-one, but, as for ourselves, we will not work for the régime of Antichrist".

' "Well then, I shall make a diagnosis for each one of you without examining you, and say you are unfit for heavy work. I shall put you all in the second category".

' "You will do no such thing. And if you do, we shall be obliged to say that what you have written isn't true. We're quite capable of working, but we do not want to work for Antichrist, and we shan't work, so they'll have to kill us".

' "They won't kill you, they'll torture you," I said; my heart was wrung with pity and my spirits very low, because I was afraid they were not listening to me.

'The youngest of the nuns said, also in a low voice, "God will help us to bear any tortures".

'A week later the the camp commandant came into the doctors' room.

' "They've really put us through it, those nuns! Now at last, in spite of everything, they've agreed to work—sewing and stitching quilts for the infirmary. But they made their own conditions, the old crows: they had to stick together and sing pslams quitely while they worked. And they were allowed to!"

'They were so completely isolated that it was a long time before we heard anything about them. It wasn't till a month later that we had any news. In one of the later convoys, a priest had been brought to Solovki who had previously been confessor to some of these nuns. And, in spite of all difficulties, they managed to get in touch with him and put themselves under his direction.

'What they told him was doubtless something like this: "We are here to suffer, but we find we are comfortable. We are together, we sing the psalms and we are doing a job after our our own hearts, making quilts for the sick. Have we done the right thing in agreeing to work under the rule of Antichrist? Would we not do better to refuse even this work?"

'The confessor replied with an absolute prohibition of work; and so the nuns refused all work. The authorities knew the source of this, and the priest was shot. But when the nuns were told of his death, they said, "Now nobody in the world can dispense us from his prohibition".

'They were separated and taken to unknown destinations. For all our efforts, we had no more news of them'.[1]

107

This episode shows us how the most ardent faith, the most severe ethic, and even the disciplines of ancient Russian spirituality (obedience to a director even after his death) were still alive in 1929. This inflexible passive resistance commanded the respect even of the secret police. There is also a story of one hundred and forty eight 'worshippers of the name of Jesus' banished to Solovki (could these have been the monks from Mount Athos deported (for heresy) in 1913?), in 1930 or a little later, who, in order to avoid serving Antichrist, refused to work and even to give their names. All were shot, with their hands tied behind their backs so that they could not make the sign of the cross.[2]

These are all monks and nuns; but examples of a similar firmness could be found among the laity as well. The Russian Church has not been without martyrs over these years. In her book, Elinor Lipper mentions some nuns who even after years of imprisonment went on refusing to work on Sundays and feast-days, and preferred to put up with hunger and physical ill-treatment. 'It was no good beating them, throwing their skirts over their heads, tying them together by their hair, nothing had any effect. The following Sunday, with the same calm, the same resolve, and the same firmness, they would get themselves sent back to their cells'.

God alone knows the numbers and the achievements of all the unknown martyrs who have suffered for their faith. A young Ukrainian girl, having been miraculously reunited with her husband, is deported a second time, once again for respecting the Lord's Day. A very old woman lets herself be dragged from one prison to another rather than deny her faith, and murmurs as the van carries her away, 'Now I have suffered almost as much as Christ. Soon my salvation will accomplished![3] It is said that the near relations of believers imprisoned for their faith will sometimes arrange to obtain copies of their interrogations and accounts of their tortures. These modern Acts of the Martyrs are reproduced in large numbers and read at secret gatherings of the faithful. At Ufa, in 1928, a certain Lydia, a secretary in the office of the Forestry Industries, duplicated some 'Acts' of this kind on a machine, and was in her turn arrested. She suffered such appalling tortures that one of the soldiers on guard, Kiril by name, fired on her two tormentors; he was himself executed. The news was later spread by another soldier, Alexei, who was also to die as a martyr.[4] This 'Golden

Legend' story seems too striking for one to dare to believe it, and it is difficult to find any proofs of its truth. But there seems no reason to suppose that there have not been practically parallel cases.

Notes

1. I have published a more complete version of this story in the review published by the Benedictines of Maredsous, *Esprit et Vie* (August, 1949, pp. 388–393). My source for it was the Russian review published in the United States. *Pravoslavnaya Rus* (29th August, 1947). Since then, partial confirmation has been supplied by Ariadna Tyrkova-Williams in the Paris journal, *Russkaya Mysl* (12th April, 1950, p. 2).
2. M. Nikonov-Smorodin, *The Red Prisons*, Sofia, 1938.
3. I take these facts from E. Lipper, *Onze ans dans les bagnes soviétiques,* Paris, 1950, pp. 73–75. 126–128. The author mentions them only in passing, as she is not specially concerned with religious matters.
4. *Pravoslavnaya Rus*, no. 12, p. 7. Since then, V. Zakharov has given an account of the life of this 'Lydia' and the triple martyrdom in question, with many more details (the fact that she was the daughter of an archpriest and received encouragement from the Archbishop of Ufa, Andrei Ukhtomsky, the circumstances of her arrest, and so on)—presented, moreover, in a most convincing manner—in *Russkaya Mysl* (31 March, 1950, pp. 4–5).

5. LEGAL POSSIBILITIES

Martyrdom, however, although it is an ultimate affirmation and, in that sense, a triumph, does not mean that the daily effort to practise religion in despite of dangers and obstacles becomes useless. We must investigate whether the Russian people have profited from the possibilities left open to them on one period or another.

Several such remained effectually open at the beginning. After the death of Patriarch Tykhon in 1925, tens of thousands of faithful felt no trepidation about going on pilgrimages to the Donskoi monastery where his body lay. In 1926, when the monastery of St Alexander Nevsky in Leningrad was given back to the patriarchal Church, a considerable sum was collected in one hour for its restoration. Everywhere those churches which are open are always full. When the authorities happen to tolerate it, a church which has been burned is soon rebuilt. A 'liquidated' church will be replaced by a hastily built wooden substitute.[1] Throughout the year, parishioners make great sacrifices to pay the ever-growing charges for insurance and repairs, and this without any hope of saving the church, simply of delaying its closure. When the monasteries were dissolved, their members grouped themselves afresh in forming communes, until the day when this camouflage would be discovered and cruelly punished. But Russia is a big place and not all local officials are equally intolerant: there are those who will close their eyes.

Here is what happened in a little Ural village in 1934. Religious life seemed to be dead; of seventeen churches, only one was left. But suddenly several believers who had been exiled returned, and a bishop who had been pardoned was allowed to live there. He was welcomed with joy: he was regularly seen doing his shopping, in his cassock and pectoral cross. The tax officer hoped to get rid of him swiftly by means of a 13,000 rouble fine: where was he likely to find that kind of money? Eight days later he paid in the complete sum. The faithful had collected it rouble by rouble.[2]

110

In the absence of a sufficient number of priests, the practice of collective confession and absolution has spread. It was a memorable sight when a whole village, deported *en bloc*, went into a church in Sergiev Posad, led by their parish priest, to receive a last absolution together.[3]

To remain thus loyal to the Church, with the certainty of imminent arrest and deportation, involved real heroism on the part of the priests, the twenty *responsables* of the parish, and the faithful in general. More important, however, the tragedy of the situation and the example of the people's loyalty led back to the Church, in its humiliation, those who had turned away from it in the days of its power. There was a movement of the intelligentsia back towards the Church: in the early days of the Revolution, several professors, writers and young people discovered a renowned *starets* at the Alexander Nevsky monastery.[4] Groups of students here and there would gather to study the Gospel and to discuss the official materialist doctrines; and these groups survived, in defiance of all denunciations, until the fatal clampdown. One of these students after his arrest was told at the GPU offices; 'You are more dangerous to us than any brigand, because we are out to prove the incompatibility of religion with science and your existence shows the opposite'.

There were even conversions among young unbelievers, members of the Young Communist League. A recent emigre relates how he discovered in his prison at Novosibirsk six former pupils of a mining school, condemned to death for an alleged conspiracy against the regime. The truth was as follows: one of them chanced one day to come across a copy of the Gospel, and read it out of sheer curiosity. He was thoroughly shaken by it, and wanted his friends too to profit from his enlightenment; five of them followed him. There is no doubt that their lives were changed by it. They were soon suspected and denounced. When arrested, they denied all false accusations but confessed their faith.[5]

As soon as the persecution seemed to be quietening down, the people were happy to show their belief. The 1936 Constitution recognised voting rights and freedom of conscience for all citizens: and immediately the Soviet press showed alarm at the amount of revived religious activity. This outcry was, of crouse, faked; it served simply to provoke and justify a new wave of arrests. However, it is thanks to this that we learn of certain very telling facts.

111

'Places of worship' began to be built again. At Donets, some miners who had obtained a grant of materials for repairing their house donated these materials to the religious association.[6] In the Magnitogorsk area, a 'cathedral' was built by the League of Militant Godless, and with the connivance of the authorities! At Volkov in the Ural district, it was the aluminium factory, the secretary of which was the president of the local League of Godless, that provided material for repairing the church.[7] Here and there there were petitions for the reopening of closed churches.[8] In rural areas, work was unashamedly suspended for feast-days, even in the full working season (and this went on for some time, as the press is still worried about it in 1939); even the saints to whom churches now closed were dedicated were commemorated.[9] The peasants organised blessings of the first fruits and processions to pray for rain. Icons reappeared in their huts.[10]

Worst of all was when the same thing happened in the collective farms. Directors of *kolkhozes* were found to be petitioning the regional authorities for permission to have all the houses in the town blessed. Not even the schools were safe: processions with crosses and banners entered schools and votive services were celebrated there.[11] In many areas, schoolchildren revived the custom of celebrating Christmas with the traditional hilarious round of the households, and they were welcomed by their schoolteachers and by members of the local Soviet.[12]

The following proves how little the persecution was the will of the people and how much the will of the authorities alone (and not even the local authorities so much as higher officialdom); it was recorded with in-dignation by *Bezbozhnik* in 1938 (no. 21): 'In the Kushva canton of the Ural district, the workers at a foundry undertook to repair their church, which was in disrepair. The fire brigade of the neighbouring village took on the expense of carrying this out. The requisite materials were collected with the help of the soldiery and the Soviet. The repairs were made, and the *responsables* of the church paid the fire brigade the sum of 2,000 roubles which they had collected. One heard of Communists who had their children baptised, and members of Young Communist groups who resigned so as to be able to have a church wedding. Finally, the clergy themselves grew bolder, and embarked on modernisation programmes. They made a great display of Soviet loyalism, celebrating thanksgiving services for the arrival of tractors in the village or perhaps the new Constitution—and exploiting this opportunity of preaching on the possibilities of action that it provided. They organised Circles of believers on the pretext of studying this Constitution.[14] In spite of the law, they engaged in religious propaganda, under the guise of choral singing, recitals of chant, theatrical productions and even football matches.[15]

Against this persistence of religious feeling, the activities of the Godless were inadequate. After a lecture on astronomy, designed to prove that God was a useless hypothesis, a worker was heard to exclaim, 'How wonderfully God has ordered the world!'[16] Confronted with educated and experienced believers, and with the questions of young people dissatisfied with the claims of materialism, the weaknesses of the official lecturers were exposed.[17] It was thought advisable not to talk too much about the Bible or the Gospel, even by way of criticism, for fear of arousing curiosity.[18]

What emerges from all this is that faith is far from dead, even among those who have submitted to enlistment in the Leagues of Godless or the Communist youth organisations.

Notes

1. This indignation of R. Martel (pp. 107–108) is aroused by some cases of this kind. I have myself come across others.
2. *Poslednie Novosti*, 7th March, 1938. I shall be making frequent quotations from this Parisian journal which reproduces information from the Soviet press with great objectivity.
3. This scene was described in Moscow, during the years of collectivisation.
4. *Pravoslavnaya Rus*, 1949, no. 8–9.
5. According to the Vienna review, *Orbis catholicus*, Nov., 1949, pp. 503–504. In speaking of students, we do not move away from considering the resistance of the people, since the students of Russia have always been very close to the people.
6. *Trud*, 27 August, 1937.
7. *Poslednie Novosti*, 5 July, 1937, following a *Pravda* report.
8. *Ibid.*, 5 June, 1937 (in the Kiev region), and 8 August, 1937.
9. *Ibid.*, 2 July, 1939 (following a report in *Bezbozhnik*, no. 18), 20

August, 1939 (*Bezbozhnik*, no. 23).

10. *Ibid.*, 8 July, 1939 (*Bezbozhnik*, no. 19).
11. *Ibid.*, 4 July, 1937 (*Sotsialisticheskoe Zemledele*, 29 June).
12. *Ibid.*, 18 April, 1939.
13. *Poslednie Novosti*, 8 July, 1939 (*Bezbozhnik*, no. 19).
14. *Poslednie Novosti*, 4 July, 1937; *Trud*, 24 September, 1937.
15. *Poslednie Novosti*, 6 July, 1937; 22 November, 1938; *Bezbozhnik*, 1938, nos. 6, 9, 21, 24, 30, and 1939, no. 4
16. Reported by Krupskaya in *Izvestia*, 27 April, 1937.
17. *Poslednie Novosti*, 2 April, 1939.
18. *Trud*, 14 December, 1938.

6. ILLEGAL OPTIONS

In spite of this, the legal possibilities were meagre and transitory. The lull of 1936 had been preceded by the great desolation of 1929–1932, and was followed by the recrudescence of persecution in 1937. The problem was how to practise religion without churches or clergy. The Russian faithful made a show of submission, but then set about discovering all kinds of new ways to satisfy their religious needs in spite of all. The relics of the saints had been taken away and displayed in antireligious museums, so one went and venerated them there, and sometimes there would be an opportunity of kissing them furtively. Monastic life was forbidden; so one took the habit secretly and kept the vows out in the world. At Solovki, in 1929 there was a man who had been chief medical officer of the Taganka prison in Moscow, Professor M. Zhizhilenko, who had been arrested for the crime of secret monastic profession; he had even been secretly consecrated a bishop.[1] Soon the Press was to delcare itself shocked by the number of monks and nuns travelling through Russia disguised as beggars and spreading 'superstition'.

Here then we come upon the existence of a clandestine clergy. Certain priests escaped arrest by taking flight; never able to settle anywhere, they travelled as cobblers, stove-builders, pedlars, or seasonal labourers, living by their work. On arriving in a district, they would collect information, and get their bearings, and then find out who the faithful were. Word would go round, and in the hut where the itinerant priest was spending the night all the religious activities people had been deprived of, perhaps for a long time, would be rapidly performed. Parents had their children baptised, couples had their marriages blessed, absolution was given, and, if there was an opporunity, Mass would be celebrated at dawn.[2]

Such itinerant priests were, of course, the most zealous and courageous ones. It was they, initially, who associated themselves with Metropolitant Pyotr. The Soviet Press several times recorded the arrest of one or other of them. '. . . Many vagabonds have been taken into custody. Among them many monks and ecclesiastics have been discovered: one such was a bishop, Sergei Druzhinin, in a village of the Mari Republic on the east bank of the Volga. The populace revered him as a saint'. Elsewhere, in Ural, a priest, Dementii, was arrested—a wealthy old peasant who had taken orders, respected even by the Communists, and regarded by the Christians as a prophet and a fool for Christ's sake.[3]

Repression naturally followed. For example, parents who had let their children be baptised were condemned for 'assault on a minor'. If these baptised children were of school age, the teacher would be accused of negligence or complicity.[4] It is thanks to such prosecutions that we are able to find out something about collective baptisms: ten or twelve here, twenty-eight there (many of them children of four to five years of age) twenty-five somewhere else (worst of all here was the fact that it took place in the house of the brother of the *kolkhoz* chairman!). At Vologda, the cemetery chapel was where children from the town, and even from the neighbouring cantons, were brought each Sunday for baptism. Even adults were baptised, according to *Bezbozhnik*.[5]

But there is not always an itinerant priest; and so the Russian peasant has other solutions. A layman of good standing will perform baptisms with water blessed by a priest, which is kept in a jar, but by aspersion only. The Soviet Press waxes very indignant over such a distortion of the Orthodox rite of immersion. For a wedding, the following procedure is adopted: one of the parents takes the two rings to the nearest priest who recites the nuptial prayers over them; and the marriage is blessed by this means.[6] For a funeral, the dead man is buried in the Soviet way, but a handful of earth taken from the grave is carried to the priest as soon as possible, together with the name of deceased; and the funeral rite is performed over this piece of earth, which is then taken back to the grave. This can also be done collectively: in the Kiev area, these handfuls of earth are collected and taken to the town; then when they have been blessed they are given to the dead man's kinsfolk who take them back and scatter them on the graves, which are thus blessed indirectly. In the Ryazan province, so it appears, two clandestine nuns even devised a way of blessing earth in advance: travellers subsequently go out into the countryside to distribute it to anyone who needs it. This practice later spread throughout the Moscow area.[7]

Legal and clandestine activity in this way mingle and complement each other. And furthermore, under an arbitrary regime, does anyone know where the frontier between the two lies?[8] It followed naturally that the faithful sometimes preferred to abandon an officially tolerated church that it was dangerous to frequent and costly to maintain, and deliberately set up a completely illegal situation. The Soviet newspapers around 1937–1939 were full of fresh alarms of this sort: a group at Murom, headed by a priest who preached the desertion of the churches and had dug catacombs where the faithful could gather beneath his house, was discovered and 'liquidated'; at Kineshma, a priest agitated for similar behaviour, declaring that it was more worthwhile to pray in one's own home; in the Ivanova region, the groups of twenty parochial 'responsables' dissolved themselves, at the instigation of the bishop, who had broken away from Sergei's jurisdiction; at Tula, a priest declared that it mattered little if the church was converted into a club: worship would be celebrated in secret.[9] Elsewhere, secret places of worship functioned in the house of a *kulak*, a deacon, and a supposedly unfrocked priest who still headed a complete religious organisation: women would bring their newborn children to him for baptism, would distribute the water blessed at Epiphany for him, and so on.

Even in the collective farms, where everyone was under surveillance, there were some who escaped: some peasants proclaimed themselves a 'brigade of Godless', and in this role they not only held aloof from the reopened church—this is immediately after the last war—but pretended to work on Sundays in a distant and difficult field. They were 'heroes of labour', thoroughgoing atheists; and among them was a clandestine priest, the pretended work on Sundays being a pretext for a private and rapid celebration of Mass.[11]

It seems that, not so very long ago, many were turning away from the officially tolerated Church, preferring secret worship, as being more pure and perhaps—as it were—more secure.[12] Whether such worship was organised with a hierarchy, whether there really was a Church of the catacombs, remains, by definition, difficult to determine. For a long time the clandestine party adhered to Metropolitan Kiril of Kazan, who died in exile in 1936. They then began to commemorate Metropolitan Iosif of Leningrad, who, as a result, was shot in 1938.[13] Other names mentioned have been those of Bishop Serafim of Yaroslavl and Bishops

117

Varlaam and Evgeny; later, those of Metropolitan Vissarion, Archbishop Grigorii of Ekaterinburg and a certain Bishop Vasilii.[14] Clandestine ordinations were performed in the Solovki camp by Bishops Maksim (the former head medical officer), Victor, Ilarion and Nektarii.[15] For further light on this matter, it would be necessary to have access to the files of the political police. What is certain is that the hierarchy did not unanimously follow Metropolitan—later Patriarch—Sergei in his complete submission to the atheistical régime.

Certainly, secret priests are rare. When, after the enthronement of the new patriarch, Alexei, in February, 1945, a new clerical body had to be constituted, it was naturally sought out in the concentration camps. Those priests who said that they recognised Alexei as head of the Church were freed and sent to parishes: the rest were kept in prison, or even shot. In any case, in many places where there were no priests, zealous laymen had gathered the faithful for prayer meetings, procured the Holy Gifts, and preserved and administered them. Sometimes this task was performed by women who had secretly made religious profession.[16] The Orthodox believer is not so disorientated by the lack of clergy as the Catholic would be, because his religious practice is less disciplined and regularised.[17] Furtheremore, even in normal times, the vast extent of the country often lays on him the necessity of doing without a church.

Illegality is still less of a novelty for the Old Believers. *Bezbozhnik* announced in September 1938 that one of their hermitages had just been discovered and destroyed in the canton of Nizhni—Tagyl in the Urals. Prayer meetings had been held there at night, under the open sky, without authorisation, under the direction of two 'leaders'. Unfortunately—the paper added—the Old Believers specialise in founding new hermitages in place of those that have been removed. Yet another illegal action of theirs was noted by the writer Fedin in *Pravda,* 16th September, 1937: in a church at Gorky (Nizhni-Novgorod), they actually dared to celebrate services together with the Orthodox. In Leningrad they had no fears about allying themselves with the 'Tykhonian' Church: a step which *Komsomolskaya Pravda* (10 September, 1937) described as an 'anti-Soviet manoeuvre'.

Nevertheless, all this underground life is not without its dangers for the purity of the faith and of worship. Many distortions are possible under such conditions, in a country where sects are already numerous and discipline is a prime necessity. We find mention somewhere of a woman—in the Caucasus, it is true— who exercised priestly functions. Sometimes there is no clear borderline between these Orthodox irregulars and not only the Old Believers but also the sects already mentioned. The Johannites, who venerated Father Ioann of Kronstadt as an incarnation of Christ, were seen to be reappearing.[18] Apocalpytic ideas often occupied an excessive place, as happens in times of persecution.[19] Equally, it is hard to say exactly what was the dogmatic content of the faith of those courageous men who declared themselves to be Christians, at the time of the 1936 census, for instance, or on the occasion of some investigation or other.[20] Some Christian schoolchildren asked about God replied, so it seems: 'God is unknown, we don't know who he is, but we feel something in our hearts', 'God is the moral order of the universe', 'God? A supreme power over and above us'—[21] answers which are not so much wrong as inadequate.

And yet, for all that, the persistance of the religious feeling and practice of the Russian people, in all its forms, legal or clandestine, seems to me to have been the conclusive factor in securing the modest space which the Church is accorded by the State at the present time. If I may express my personal opinion in reply to the question posed above, it is the people who, by their Christian perseverance and often heroic faith, have obtained this respite—far more, surely, than the compromise policy of the higher ranks among the official clergy.[22] We may say that, on the human level, the main reason for the preservation of Christianity in Russia was the impossibility of destroying man's need for religion. After more than half a century of persecution the like of which has never been seen, mounted by an all-powerful State with every available material and ideological means, the religion of Christ still exists in Russia; and this is something which confounds the understanding, and demands explanation on a higher level. That visionary philosopher, Vladimir Soloviev, said to his friend Velichko shortly before his death: 'I feel that the day is coming when Christians will again be gathering for prayer in the catacombs, because the faith will be persecuted—perhaps in a less violent way than in the days of Nero, but with greater refinements of cruelty: lies, mockery, falsification, and many other things again . . . Do you not see who is coming? I have seen him for a long time now . . .[23] Was what he saw the battle ordained by Providence between Christ and Antichrist?

Notes

1. *Pravoslavnaya Rus*, 1947, no. 13, p. 9; 1951, no. 1, p. 6.
2. *Ekonomicheskaya Zhizn*, no. 142, One such priest was discovered at the port of Baku, disguised as a boatswain.
3. *Trud*, 15 April, 1937; *Sotsialisticheskoe Zemledelie*, 11th January, 1938; *Bezbozhnik*, 21 April, 1939; *Poslednie Novosti*, July, 1938.
4. *Komsomolskaya Pravda*, 27th March, 1938.
5. 1938, no. 4; 11 April and 21 July, 1939. Things had not changed in 1961 (*Literaturnaya Gazeta*, 1961, no. 11): 'Every three months a priest arrives—nobody knows where from—to baptise children born in his absence, hear confessions and strengthen the faith of the believers. His propaganda is most effective: its results are immediately obvious'.
6. *Poslednie Novosti*, 1939, 23 and 25 June. There is an analogous account in *Antireligioznik*, 1940, no. 2, pp. 24–28.
7. *Bezbozhnik*, 1938, nos. 14 and 20; 1939, nos. 12 and 19; *Poslednie Novosti*, 30 June, 1939.
8. Official propaganda in 1937 made a great deal out of a monstrous case in which the bishop of Orel, twelve priests, three deacons, two nuns and a dozen laymen were prosecuted. The charges (apart from counter-revolutionary conspiracy) were under these heads: general confessions heard by an archpriest, secondment of priests banned from the towns to rural churches, incitement of the faithful to request the reopening of churches, baptisms of children of school age, confessions in the priest's home, and borrowing of working methods from the Catholic clergy. Not one of these activities was strictly illegal (Anderson, pp. 112–115).
9. *Bezbozhnik*, 1938, nos. 21, 26, 27.
10. *Bezbozhnik*, 1938, nos. 3, 10, 31; *Poslednie Novosti*, 12 November, 1938.
11. *Pravoslavnaya Rus*, 1949.
12. A young man in the Urals in the autumn of 1948 declared: 'Nowadays you only trust a priest in lay clothes, without a beard. If he

has a beard and a cassock, and specially if he wears an expensive cross, he can only be a police agent'. (*Russkaya Mysl*, Supplement to no. 183, October, 1949).

13. *Pravoslavnaya Rus*, 1951, no. 1, p. 8.
14. *Pravda*, 2 March, 1937; *Bezbozhnik*, 1938, nos. 3 and 4 and 1939, no. 1; *Poslednie Novosti*, January, 1939.
15. *Pravoslavnaya Rus*, 1951, no. 1, p. 8.
16. Report read on 7 December, 1950, before the Synod of the Russian Orthodox Church in Exile (Metropolitan Anastasii's jurisdiction), reproduced in *Pravoslavnaya Rus*, no. 1, pp. 8–10.
17. However, during the French Revolution too there were attempts at organising an underground Church: see Ch. Ledré, *Le culte caché sous la revolution*, Paris, 1949.
18. *Poslednie Novosti*, 28th July, 1938, and 12 February, 1939.
19. *Bezozhnik*, 1939, no. 20; *Antireligionznik*, 1939, no. 5. We have already seen above nuns refusing to 'work for Antichrist'.
20. In investigation conducted among the peasants (not yet living in collective farms) of the canton of Novozhersk, in the Tver province, in 1933, established that all had preserved their icons, three-quarters believed in miracles, the same number thought that religion did not interfere at all with their jobs, and 83% had never read any antireligious publication (*Antireligioznik*, 1933, Sept.–Oct.).
21. *Antireligioznik, ibid.*
22. That 15% among the young soldiers of a cavalry regiment, who declared themselves still to be believers after being subjected under orders to a year's intensive activity by forty Militant Godless (conferences, films, etc.), must have been Christians indeed! (*Antireligioznik*, 1931, no. 1, p. 60).
23. In 1898, Soloviev had published his *Three Dialogues*, including the 'Tale of Antichrist'. He died on 31 July, 1900. The reminiscences of V. L. Velichko, *Vladimir Soloviev, his Life and Works*, appeared at St Petersburg in 1902.

.

EPILOGUE

The plan of this brief work, as will already have been remarked, is as follows. The first part of the text deals with the religion of the Russian people in a more or less timeless style; but all cases considered are in fact from the period before 1917. The third part observes the same religion confronted by the persecution unleashed by the Revolution, up to the time of Russia's entry into the last war. The second part presents, essentially, the answer which the Russian religious consciousness, not long after its first meeting with Christianity, desired to give to the problem of evil.

The reader will, I hope, recognise that the contemporary fact of the people's remarkable resistance to this war to the death being waged against the structures, faith and practice of Christianity can be very largely explained by the general traits which I attempted to define in my opening section. The moral and physical destruction of the clergy was of much less consequence to a laity well used to asking little of its priests. The prohibition of dogmatic instruction has not seriously touched a religion which is more moral than intellectual, transmitted less through catechisms than through family tradition. Evangelical faith can maintain itself even without printed gospels. Even the destruction of churches, so desolating in that it deprived the people of the splendours of the liturgy, had not so radical an effect when there was a living saint, a fool for Christ or a martyr, at hand for veneration. Where there was a church, the freedom permitted, narrow as this was, for worship—with liturgy, choirs, icons and a little preaching—was enough to maintain religion among a people who drew whatever was most clearly defined in their Christianity from this liturgy. And finally, if suffering for the faith seemed necessary, was not imposed suffering, even without the sacraments, a pledge of salvation?

This popular Russian religion, which I have been at pains to distinguish from the religion of the cultivated classes, is what I have attempted to define; doubtless I shall be rebuked for having idealised it. But I do not pretend that this was the religion of every man among the people: the traits I have described are those which I have most commonly observed among the most genuinely religious of the people. The rest have provided us with no material, and I have not been concerned with them.

Finally, although popular Russian religion may have its originality I had no intention of presenting it in opposition to that of Western peoples of the Catholic Church. Indeed, it is precisely on the level of the simple believer that the separation between the two Churches, the Eastern and the Western, is least important. On the contrary, I should like to draw attention to some particularly striking similarities between popular religion on both sides of the separation.

Let us take the characteristically Russian emphasis on demonstrative religion, the abundance of outward signs of piety—kissing of images, repeated signs of the cross, prostrations, tears. Our modern piety discreetly avoids, to an ever-increasing extent, any 'exteriorisation', for many reasons. But throughout the centuries, prayer with tears, for instance, has been a regular practice—natural tears, not by any means necessarily tears of compunction, but of heartfelt tenderness as well. There is Saint Geneviève, the shepherdess: 'every time she looked at the sky when she was praying, her eyes would fill with tears'. Saint Catherine of Siena, after receiving the host, would break into sobbing. In the seventeenth century, in the Life of Mère de Ponçonas, we hear of a cow-girl who never succeeded in saying the Lord's Prayers: 'When I say the word "Pater",' she confided to Mère de Ponçonas, 'and I think . . . that he who is on high . . . is my father . . . I weep and don't stop for the whole day'. Even in the last century, the Curé d'Ars—a simple countryman himself—would weep as he said Mass. Scholars too, and even theologians, who wrote about 'affective devotion' and the 'gift of tears', knew how to weep. The Roman Missal has three prayers *propetitione lacrimarum*. It is only in relatively recent times that attitudes—if not hearts—have hardened.

Or take another very Russian trait, pity for the 'unfortunate', that is, condemned criminals. The Italian writer Silone in his *Uscita di sicurezza* (1965) tell us of a child of Abruzzi who saw an unhappy man hobbling along between two policemen, and said to his father, 'Look at that funny

124

man!' The father gave him a stern look and tweaked his ear: 'You never make fun of prisoners', he said, 'Never!' 'Why?' 'Because they can't defend themselves. And then, they may be innocent. But in any case, you don't because they are unfortunates'. This trait seems to be drawn from life (perhaps it is autobiographical). Everything is here—both scepticism about human justice, and Christian pity.

It would be pointless to mention pilgrimage, which at one time involved the same sacrifices and risks in the West as in Russia—the same pulling-up of domestic roots, the same accompaniment of beggars and indigents with their pious laments. In Florence during Holy Week, I once heard a man in the forecourt of the Duomo begging for alms by chanting the very same narrative of the Passion as that used by the singers of 'spiritual songs' in the Lavra at Kiev.

The 'fool for Christ' might be taken for a uniquely Russian or Eastern phenomenon. But the Catholic West has never been lacking in souls avid for abjection out of humility, penitence, or the desire to imitate Christ. We must make some distinctions, however. There are those great saints who have at times practised the folly of the Cross—Francis of Assisi, Philip Neri, Ignatius Loyola, or, in our own day, Père de Foucauld, who used to collect dung in the streets of Nazareth, so as to provoke the mockery of the little Arab boys, who threw stones at him. Many other such could be cited, but they do not play quite the same role as do the Russian fools for Christ. Real kinsfolk of the latter were the *pazzi di Cristo*, who abounded in tumultuous sixteenth century Siena. Brandano, a peasant, converted after a misspent youth by an accident, was a true fool for Christ, who desired to suffer as Christ did: on one occasion he had himself hung on a cross. He would walk around barefoot, ragged and long-haired, lacerating his breast with a sharp stone, or carrying a heavy cross. He invited ill-treatment and beatings. He cared nothing for the authorities, preaching without licence and abusing unsatisfactory priests. When Siena was in danger, besieged by the united forces of the Pope and of the Florentines, he became tribune of the town. When the victory was won, he went off to Rome to rebuke the Pope, throwing a handful of bones at his feet with the words, 'Think on death!' Some time later, when the Pope expelled the first Capuchins from Rome, Brandano cried out among the crowds, 'Wicked men and criminals flock to Rome, while the good and virtuous are exiled from it!'

125

Later still, Siena was under the control of a Spanish governor, Don Diego de Mendoza, who was supervising the building of a castle to guard the town. Brandano came along, singing the psalm *Nisi Dominus*: 'Except the Lord build the house, their labour is but lost that build it: except the Lord keep the city, the watchman waketh but in vain'. Here is the fool as defender of the city, reminding anyone who violates its liberty of the existence of a higher order. In the same way—and at almost the same time—Nikolai Klopsky saved Pskov, making Ivan the Terrible himself tremble. These Western fools for Christ, like their Russian counterparts, were sometimes privileged to play a prophetic role in hammering home, to populace and rulers alike, truths that no-one else had the courage—or perhaps the talent—to express.

And finally, it would be wrong to think that the idea of the Mother of God's intercession for the damned had not affected popular Western piety. In Italy (in Umbria in fact) there used to be a hymn sung on the Sundays in Advent which represented the damned beseeching Christ for pardon. The archangel Gabriel and all the elect plead on their behalf against Satan. Christ as sovereign judge reminds the accursed of their sins: 'You have seen me hungry and thirsty . . . and gave me nothing to eat or drink. I was a wanderer . . . going naked on my way, and you turned your heads from me. I was sick, I was a prisoner . . .' The damned attempt to justify themselves: 'Lord, when we saw you afflicted with so many ills, we knew nothing of your distress'. And the reply comes from the judge: 'Whenever a poor man asked alms of you, I was in him. With each sin you crucified me. And yet I waited for you tenderly, hoping to spare you. Now away with you, accursed folk!' The sinners then turn to Mary, who attempts to change her Son's mind: 'For the sake of the milk I fed you with, listen to me a little while, my Son, and forgive those for whom I plead . . . Nine months I bore you in my virginal womb, and you drank from these breasts when you were a little child. I beg you, if it be possible, wipe out your sentence'. Emil Gebhart, who quotes this moving hymn in his *Italie mystique,* does not, unfortunately, tell us the outcome of the debate; but is clear enough that the thirteenth century Umbrian Catholic writer was inspired by the same feelings that moved the Orthodox Kievan translator of the *Pilgrimage of the Mother of God*.

Generally, it is a great mistake to seek to put Orthodox and Catholic spirituality in opposition to each other. People think for instance, of the

Russian Church as entirely mystical and unconcerned with this world, and the Catholic Church as preoccupied above all with this world, to the point of forgetting about Heaven. But this is to ignore, on the one side, St Francis of Assisi, St John of the Cross, and many more; and, on the other, those metropolitans canonised for their part in building up the Muscovite State side by side with the Grand Dukes. People think of Orthodoxy as concentrating entirely on the Resurrection, and Catholicism as concentrating on the humanity of Christ and the Passion; although it is Orthodoxy that has the longer and more severe Lenten fast, and never fails to revere the imitation of Christ on the part of its saints, and Catholicism which devotes the most magnificent office of all its liturgy to Paschaltide.

In reality, the differences which appear to exist between the two Churches especially on the level of popular religion, are by no means absolute; it is a question of the same features existing on both sides, but in different proportions; which is quite normal, since the source is the same, although the conditions of life are different. Again, if one studies popular religion, in France for instance, prior to the Council of Trent, or even up to the end of the seventeenth century (when the Council had yet to make its effects properly felt), one finds it very close to that of Russia before 1917. In France too, beliefs had not yet been precisely defined in catechetical teaching, but still depended on family tradition; they were less a matter of intellect, more a matter of feeling, than they later became; the practice of religion also was at once more free and more bound up with daily life, and so more closely related to the sorrows and joys of everyday work, and more closely related to nature. There was an elaborate cult of the saints, processions to petition for the fruits of the earth or for the cessation of a plague. The believer was more aware of his dependence on Providence, and, equally, more aware of the menace of the Devil. Between him and his priests there was not as yet the barrier cast up by a great difference in education and behaviour. Only in the second half of the seventeenth century were rational order and regularity introduced, and the people's religion assimilated to that of the theologians and the literate classes. A parallel evolution has now taken place in Italy, though the examples quoted above show that it began rather later on; in certain areas, its progress is still a good deal slower.

These correspondences suggest that when a country abandons rural life and crafts, a way of life that is communitarian and intuitive, to embark upon an urban existence, nationally organised, and preoccupied with rational, moral and prudential considerations, popular religion evolves along the same lines. Thus the religion of the Russian people, as I have described it, with its libertarian and evangelical character, is not peculiar to one particular race or one particular Church; it is the sign of a particular epoch of civilisation—however sad a conclusion this may be for the Slavophil, or for any other narrow nationalist.

GLOSSARY

akathist: a long liturgical poem.

antimins: (from the Greek *antimension*) a piece of cloth about eighteen inches square which covers the altar during the celebration of the Orthodox Liturgy; relics are sewn into it, and it must be consecrated by a bishop.

artel: a society of labourers or artisans.

bashlyk: the head of an *artel*.

doulia (hyperdoulia and **latria):** according to the Seventh Ecumenical Council, **doulia** is the type of worship given to icons, **hyperdoulia** is the worship given to the Mother of God, while **latria**, the highest level, is reserved for God alone.

Ioann of Kronstadt: Fr Ioann Sergeiev (1829–1908), a noted spiritual director, writer and preacher, with a reputation for performing miraculous cures.

izba: a peasant's hut.

izvochnik: a carrier or cabdriver.

kasha: gruel.

khlysty: a Russian sect of flagellants.

lapti: bast shoes.

Lent, 'St Peter's: several feast-days (including the Assumption and Saints Peter and Paul) in the Orthodox Church are preceded by periods of fasting and abstinence; 'St Peter's Lent' is thus simply the fast preceding the feast of Saints Peter and Paul. The pre-Easter period is referred to as the 'great fast' or 'Great Lent'.

moleben: a short service of thanksgiving.

muzhik: a peasant, rustic.

Nikon, Nikonians: Nikon, Patriarch of Moscow from 1652 to 1666, was the leading figure in the attempt to bring the ritual of the Russian Church into line with that of the Greek-speaking Orthodox; this attempt provoked a serious schism, and the adherents of the 'official

129

party which followed the Patriarch were long referred to as Nikonians' by the schismatics.

Old Believers: the general name for those who refused to accept Nikon's reforms; their most articulate apologist was the Archpriest Avvakum, the anthor of a justly celebrated autobiography. One group among the Old Believers, the *bezpopovtsy* or 'priestless', has had no clergy since the schism. All the schismatics were persecuted very harshly by successive Tsars, and exiled in large numbers to the sparsely-populated areas east of the Volga.

Pechersky Lavra: the Monastery of the Caves at Kiev, the oldest monastic foundation in Russia.

skoptsy: a Russian sect practising self-castration.

Stoglav: the Council of the 'Hundred Chapters', convened at Moscow in 1551 by Ivan the Terrible, which issued condemnations of abuses in monasteries and parishes, and initiated significant reforms in the Russian Church.

Synod of the Russian Orthodox Church in Exile: one of the four jurisdictions existing among the Russian *émigrés*; traditionalist in theology, and profoundly anti-ecumenical, it regards the Soviet régime as Antichrist, and consequently considers the Moscow Patriarchate as having forfeited all canonical authority by its compromises with the Marxist State. It is quite strong in the USA, where it produces several substantial publications.

Troitsa-Sergei: the Monastery of the Trinity and St Sergius at Zagorsk, near Moscow, founded by Sergei of Radonezh in the fourteenth century, and still one of the most popular centres of pilgrimage in Russia.